# KEY TO
# KOREAN
# DAILY BASIC
# CONVERSATION
## : 75 MUST-KNOW SENTENCE PATTERNS

교육 R&D에 앞서가는
 키출판사

# GUIDE TO THIS BOOK

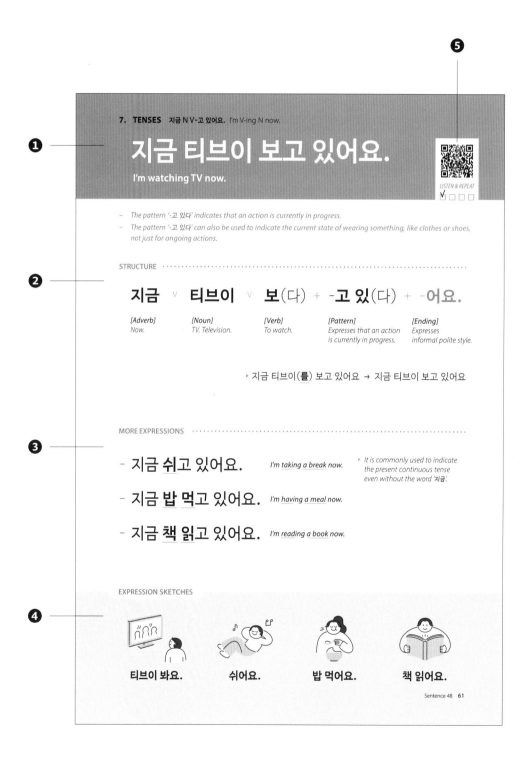

**❶**

**7. TENSES** 지금 N V-고 있어요. I'm V-ing N now.

# 지금 티브이 보고 있어요.
**I'm watching TV now.**

LISTEN & REPEAT

- The pattern '-고 있다' indicates that an action is currently in progress.
- The pattern '-고 있다' can also be used to indicate the current state of wearing something, like clothes or shoes, not just for ongoing actions.

STRUCTURE

**❷**

지금 ∨ 티브이 ∨ 보(다) + -고 있(다) + -어요.

| | | | | |
|---|---|---|---|---|
| *[Adverb]* | *[Noun]* | *[Verb]* | *[Pattern]* | *[Ending]* |
| Now. | TV. Television. | To watch. | Expresses that an action is currently in progress. | Expresses informal polite style. |

▸ 지금 티브이(를) 보고 있어요 → 지금 티브이 보고 있어요

MORE EXPRESSIONS

**❸**

- 지금 **쉬고** 있어요.   *I'm taking a break now.*   ▸ It is commonly used to indicate the present continuous tense even without the word '지금'.

- 지금 **밥 먹고** 있어요.   *I'm having a meal now.*

- 지금 **책 읽고** 있어요.   *I'm reading a book now.*

EXPRESSION SKETCHES

**❹**

티브이 봐요.     쉬어요.     밥 먹어요.     책 읽어요.

Sentence 48   61

## STEP 1. MAIN BOOK

### ① *The Essential Key Sentence*

These sentences are commonly used in daily life and essential to know. You can use them in everyday conversations.

The lists provided by official institutions were used to extract common patterns and words.

### ② *Sentence Structure at a Glance*

Korean grammar is easy.

There are just a few 'particles' and 'endings' between words. Once you understand the rules for using them, you can make and say as many as sentences you want.

### ③ *Sentence Expansion*

Learning one sentence is not enough.

Learn additional sentences you can use as alternatives; combine, or change a word. This makes understanding the key sentence easier without memorization.

### ④ *Customized Additional Activities*

For each key sentence, we provide extra materials like pictures, dialogs, and short explanations. These activities can thoroughly guide and help with learning.

+

### « *KOREAN NATIVE VIBE TIPS* »

Each chapter ends with unique, essential tips. These tips are helpful for mastering real-life conversations, helping you speak like a native.

## STEP 2. MULTIMEDIA

### ⑤ *Accurate Sentence Pronunciation*

Practice pronunciation accuracy by listening to audio files recorded by professional voice actors. This helps you easily understand where to pause and how to pronounce linked sounds. You can also listen to the whole chapter's audio in one file on the QR page.

## STEP 3. WORKBOOK

### ⑥ *Activities for Perfect Finish*

It's different from just reading good content.

Strengthen what you've learned with activities in the workbook. This helps you practice the key sentences and use them yourself.

# TABLE OF CONTENTS

# STUDY PLAN

*Write the Date, Learn and Check **3 Sentences a Day**! Complete **in 25 Days**!*
*- One sentence: One on each page of the Main Book, Multimedia, and Workbook.*

| DAY 1 | DAY 2 | DAY 3 | DAY 4 | DAY 5 |
|---|---|---|---|---|
| ____월 ____일 | ____월 ____일 | ____월 ____일 | ____월 ____일 | ____월 ____일 |
| Sentence 1 ☐ | Sentence 4 ☐ | Sentence 7 ☐ | Sentence 10 ☐ | Sentence 13 ☐ |
| Sentence 2 ☐ | Sentence 5 ☐ | Sentence 8 ☐ | Sentence 11 ☐ | Sentence 14 ☐ |
| Sentence 3 ☐ | Sentence 6 ☐ | Sentence 9 ☐ | Sentence 12 ☐ | Sentence 15 ☐ |
| DAY 6 | DAY 7 | DAY 8 | DAY 9 | DAY 10 |
| ____월 ____일 | ____월 ____일 | ____월 ____일 | ____월 ____일 | ____월 ____일 |
| Sentence 16 ☐ | Sentence 19 ☐ | Sentence 22 ☐ | Sentence 25 ☐ | Sentence 28 ☐ |
| Sentence 17 ☐ | Sentence 20 ☐ | Sentence 23 ☐ | Sentence 26 ☐ | Sentence 29 ☐ |
| Sentence 18 ☐ | Sentence 21 ☐ | Sentence 24 ☐ | Sentence 27 ☐ | Sentence 30 ☐ |
| DAY 11 | DAY 12 | DAY 13 | DAY 14 | DAY 15 |
| ____월 ____일 | ____월 ____일 | ____월 ____일 | ____월 ____일 | ____월 ____일 |
| Sentence 31 ☐ | Sentence 34 ☐ | Sentence 37 ☐ | Sentence 40 ☐ | Sentence 43 ☐ |
| Sentence 32 ☐ | Sentence 35 ☐ | Sentence 38 ☐ | Sentence 41 ☐ | Sentence 44 ☐ |
| Sentence 33 ☐ | Sentence 36 ☐ | Sentence 39 ☐ | Sentence 42 ☐ | Sentence 45 ☐ |
| DAY 16 | DAY 17 | DAY 18 | DAY 19 | DAY 20 |
| ____월 ____일 | ____월 ____일 | ____월 ____일 | ____월 ____일 | ____월 ____일 |
| Sentence 46 ☐ | Sentence 49 ☐ | Sentence 52 ☐ | Sentence 55 ☐ | Sentence 58 ☐ |
| Sentence 47 ☐ | Sentence 50 ☐ | Sentence 53 ☐ | Sentence 56 ☐ | Sentence 59 ☐ |
| Sentence 48 ☐ | Sentence 51 ☐ | Sentence 54 ☐ | Sentence 57 ☐ | Sentence 60 ☐ |
| DAY 21 | DAY 22 | DAY 23 | DAY 24 | DAY 25 |
| ____월 ____일 | ____월 ____일 | ____월 ____일 | ____월 ____일 | ____월 ____일 |
| Sentence 61 ☐ | Sentence 64 ☐ | Sentence 67 ☐ | Sentence 70 ☐ | Sentence 73 ☐ |
| Sentence 62 ☐ | Sentence 65 ☐ | Sentence 68 ☐ | Sentence 71 ☐ | Sentence 74 ☐ |
| Sentence 63 ☐ | Sentence 66 ☐ | Sentence 69 ☐ | Sentence 72 ☐ | Sentence 75 ☐ |

# KEY TO KOREAN DAILY BASIC CONVERSATION

## Basic Korean knowledge to know:

*Korean builds sentences using 'particles' and 'endings' between words.*

- *Particle: Particles are attached to nouns, adverbs, endings, etc., to show grammatical relationships or add special meanings.*

- *Ending: Endings are added after a verb or an adjective to express honorifics, tense, questions, and other intentions of the speaker.*

- *Honorifics: Korean shows different levels of respect using words, particles, and endings. This textbook uses the most common endings for honorifics.*

- *Some particles or endings can have the same function, but their forms may change depending on the form of the preceding word.*

## Regarding this textbook:

- *The English translations next to the Korean sentences are often literal to keep nuances, which may sound unnatural.*

- *Check the <STRUCTURE> to see how two characters often contract into one, especially when a character without a final consonant meets a vowel. Here, particles and endings are indicated with colored letters.*

- *For particles and endings that change depending on the preceding letter, see the <GRAMMAR RECAP> on page 94, which shows the forms used in different cases.*

- *Abbreviations used: N for Nouns, V for Verbs, A for Adjectives, Adv for Adverbs.*

# 안녕하세요?

### Hello?

LISTEN & REPEAT

- *This is the most common greeting when you meet someone. The usual response is not to share how you're actually doing, but to simply reply with '안녕하세요?'*
- *The ending '-시-' expresses honorific, and the sentence-closing ending '-어요' expresses informal polite style.*

## STRUCTURE

### 안녕하(다) + -시- + -어요?

*[Adjective]*
*To be healthy*
*and peaceful.*

*[Ending]*
*Expresses*
*honorific.*

*[Ending]*
*Expresses*
*informal polite style.*

▸ 안녕하**시어**요 → 안녕하**세**요

## MORE EXPRESSIONS

- 반갑습니다.

  Nice to meet you.

  ▸ *These are greetings you can use to warmly welcome someone when meeting them for the first time.*

- 처음 뵙겠습니다.

  Pleased to meet you.

- 말씀 많이 들었습니다.

  *I've heard a lot about you.*

## EXPRESSIVE TIPS

### 안녕?

*[Informal Casual Style]*
*Used with someone younger or of a similar age who is very close to you. Avoid using this form solely based on someone being younger, as it can be considered rude.*

### 안녕하세요?

*[Informal Polite Style]*
*The most common greeting for everyone, from strangers to close acquaintances.*

### 안녕하십니까?

*[Formal Polite Style]*
*Appropriate for public or official contexts. This form can be used with co-workers or people you meet in public settings.*

# 감사합니다.

**Thank you.**

LISTEN & REPEAT

– Among greetings, the formal polite style(-ㅂ니다/-습니다) tends to be more commonly used than the informal polite style(-아/어/해요).
– While '감사해요.' is acceptable, '감사합니다.' is more common and considered more polite.

## STRUCTURE ········································································

### 감사하(다)  +  -ㅂ니다.

[Adjective]
To appreciate,
to be thankful.

[Ending]
Expresses
formal polite style.

▸ 감사**하ㅂ**니다 → 감사**합**니다

## MORE EXPRESSIONS ········································································

– **고맙습니다.**     *Thank you.*     ▸ *It is used in more casual or everyday situations than '감사합니다.'*

– **고마워요.**     *Thanks.*     ▸ *It is used in an informal polite style, only towards peers or those younger.*

– **아니에요.**     *Don't mention it.*     ▸ *It literally means 'It's not.'*
▸ *Responses to '감사합니다.' include '아니에요.', '괜찮아요(It's fine).' You can use them individually or together.*

## DIALOG GLIMPSES

### 감사합니다.
*Thank you.*

### 아니에요. 괜찮아요.
*Don't mention it. It's fine.*

# 죄송합니다.

**I'm sorry.**

LISTEN & REPEAT

- This expression is widely used and can be used for not only big mistakes but also small things like stepping on someone's foot.
- Responses to this can be exactly the same as those to '감사합니다.' such as '아니에요.', '괜찮아요.'

## STRUCTURE

### 죄송하(다)  +  -ㅂ니다.

[Adjective]
To be sorry.

[Ending]
Expresses
formal polite style.

▸ 죄송<u>하ㅂ</u>니다 → 죄송<u>합</u>니다

## MORE EXPRESSIONS

- 실례합니다.  *Excuse me.*

- 미안해요.  *I'm sorry.*  ▸ *'미안해요.' or '미안합니다.' is a lighter expression than '죄송합니다.', and only towards peers or those younger.*

- 괜찮아요.  *It's okay.*  ▸ *'괜찮다' means 'to be fine'.*

## EXPRESSIVE TIPS

*When you hear "**죄송합니다.**" in situations like being bumped into or having your foot stepped on, it's okay to simply nod or just say "**네**(Yes)." briefly.*
*Of course, you can also say "**아니에요, 괜찮아요.**", but in reality, people often just respond briefly.*

# 잘 먹겠습니다.

**Thank you for the meal.**

LISTEN & REPEAT
✓ ☐ ☐ ☐

- This expression is used before meals; literally translated as 'I will eat well,' but it shows thanks and enjoyment for the food.
- The ending '-겠-' expresses subject's will. When the subject is not specified, it's typically assumed to be 'I'.

STRUCTURE ·····················································

**잘** ∨ **먹**(다) + **-겠-** + **-습니다.**

| | | | |
|---|---|---|---|
| *[Adverb]* | *[Verb]* | *[Ending]* | *[Ending]* |
| Well. | To eat. | Expresses subject's will. | Expresses formal polite style. |

▸ 잘 먹겠습니다

MORE EXPRESSIONS ·····································

— **맛있게 드세요.**  *Enjoy your meal.*  ▸ *The person who made the food can say this, and so can someone eating with you.*

— **잘 먹었습니다.**  *Thank you for the meal.*  ▸ *This is said after eating. The one letter '-었-' means the past tense.*
▸ *You can also say this to the staff when leaving a restaurant.*

— **배불러요.**  *I'm full.*

EXPRESSION SKETCHES

# 안녕히 계세요.

**Goodbye.**

LISTEN & REPEAT

- *This goodbye is said by the person leaving. '계시다' means 'to stay' respectfully.*
- *If both people are leaving, you can say '안녕히 가세요.' '가시다' means 'to go' respectfully.*

## STRUCTURE

### 안녕히 ∨ 계시(다) + -어요.

**[Adverb]**
*In peace.*

**[Verb]**
*The honorific of '있다(To be/exist).'*

**[Ending]**
*Expresses informal polite style.*

▸ 안녕히 계**시어**요 → 안녕히 계**세**요

## MORE EXPRESSIONS

- **안녕히 가세요.**    *Goodbye.*    ▸ *It's a goodbye from the person staying to the person leaving.*

- **다음에 봐요.**    *See you later.*    ▸ *'뵈다' is the honorific of '보다(to see).'*
  ▸ 뵈(다) + -어요 → 뵈어요 → 봬요

- **좋은 하루 보내세요.**    *Have a nice day.*

## DIALOG GLIMPSES

**안녕히 계세요.**
*Goodbye.*

**네, 안녕히 가세요.**
*You, too. Goodbye.*

## 1.  GREETINGS

# 잘 지내셨어요?

**Have you been well?**

*LISTEN & REPEAT*
☑ ☐ ☐ ☐

- *It's a commonly used expression when asking how someone has been after not seeing them for a long time.*
- *In Korean, the subject 'you' is often omitted when speaking about the person directly in front of you.*

### STRUCTURE · · · · · · · · · · · · · · · · · · · · · · · · · · · · · · · · · · · · · · · · · · · · · · ·

**잘** ∨ **지내**(다) + **-시-** + **-었-** + **-어요?**

| | | | | |
|---|---|---|---|---|
| *[Adverb]* | *[Verb]* | *[Ending]* | *[Ending]* | *[Ending]* |
| *Well.* | *To live or go on in a certain state.* | *Expresses honorific.* | *Expresses the past tense.* | *Expresses informal polite style.* |

▸ 잘 지내**시었**어요 → 잘 지내**셨**어요

### MORE EXPRESSIONS · · · · · · · · · · · · · · · · · · · · · · · · · · · · · · · · · · · · · · · · ·

- **뭐 하고 지내셨어요?**     *What have you been up to?*

- **오랜만이에요.**     *Long time no see.*

- **보고 싶었어요.**     *I missed you.*

### EXPRESSIVE TIPS

*The sentences from this page are greetings for when you meet someone you already know after a long time, not for the first time. It's okay to respond briefly instead of explaining in detail what you have been up to.*

*If the person is the same age or younger and there's no need to be very formal, you can omit the honorific ending '-시-' and ask* **"잘 지냈어요?"** *or* **"뭐 하고 지냈어요?"**

# 저는 마이클이에요.

I'm Michael.

LISTEN & REPEAT
✓ ☐ ☐ ☐

- It's the most basic sentence form in the informal polite style for talking about 'I' with a noun.
- '이다' is attached after a noun to describe it.

## STRUCTURE

저 + 는 ∨ 마이클 + 이(다) + -에요.

**[Pronoun]**
The humble
form of '나(I)'.

**[Particle]**
Indicates the topic
of the sentence.

**[Noun]**
Michael.

Attached after a noun
to describe it.

**[Ending]**
Expresses
informal polite style.

▸ 저는 마이클이에요

## MORE EXPRESSIONS

- 저는 **미국 사람**이에요.  I'm _American._  ▸ You just need to attach your country's name in front of '사람(person)' to express your nationality.

- 저는 **김지수**예요.  I'm _Jisoo Kim._  ▸ When the letter preceding '이에요' ends in a vowel, '이에요' is shortened to '예요'.

- 저는 **여자**예요.  I'm _a woman._  ▸ 'Man' is '남자'.

## EXPRESSIVE TIPS

A basic Korean sentence ends with either **'Verb/adjective + Ending'** or **'Noun + 이다/아니다(to be/ to not be) + Ending'**. In this book, most sentences will be presented with the most commonly used informal polite ending. The '이에요/예요' following a noun, is a form of '이다' combined with an informal polite ending '-에요'.
We've covered basic greetings in this chapter. Let's learn verbs, adjectives, endings, particles etc., from the next chapter onwards, so you can speak the sentences you want to say.

# What do Koreans say instead of "Excuse me."?

*While "Excuse me." is often translated to '***실례합니다***.' in Korean, the phrase "***실례합니다***." is rarely used in daily conversation. It is more common in formal settings or among older people. In Korea, different expressions are used for different situations.*

*To start a conversation with strangers, it's common to begin with "***저기요****(Hey)." or "****저, 혹시*** (Well, by any chance)…" before continuing. It's fine to be specific, like "***저, 길 좀 여쭐게요****(Well, may I ask for directions?)." to ask for directions. In busy areas like downtown Gangnam, people might be cautious of strangers because of street promoters or religious campaigners. It's helpful to explain your intent from the beginning.*

*To move through a crowd, phrases like "***잠시만요****(Just a moment)." or "****지나갈게요****(I'll get through)." are used to ask people to make way. These phrases are essential in crowded places, like packed subways or buses, especially when you need to exit.*

*If you accidentally bump into someone or step on their foot, using "***죄송합니다****(I'm sorry)." is appropriate.*

*In restaurants, it's usual to catch a server's attention with eye contact or a slight hand raise. If you need to call out, you can say "***여기요****(Here, please)." or directly state your need like "****주문이요****(Order, please)." or "****주문할게요****(I'd like to order)." is common. In Korea, it is also fine to call out to a staff member as long as you show a polite attitude.*

## 2. PARTICLES ① N은/는 잘 지내요? Is N doing well?

# 오빠는 잘 지내요?
**Is your older brother doing well?**

LISTEN & REPEAT

- *This expression asks about someone's well-being. In Korean, the word order in a question stays the same. You can make a question by adding a question mark and raising your intonation at the end of the sentence.*
- *The particle '은/는' is attached after the topic of the sentence.*

## STRUCTURE

**오빠** + **는** ∨ **잘** ∨ **지내(다)** + **-어요?**

*[Noun]*
Older brother.

*[Particle]*
Indicates the topic of the sentence.

*[Adverb]*
Well.

*[Verb]*
To live or go on in a certain state.

*[Ending]*
Expresses informal polite style.

▸ 오빠는 잘 지**내어**요 → 오빠는 잘 지**내**요

## MORE EXPRESSIONS

- **언니는 잘 지내요?**    *Is your older sister doing well?*

- **동생은 잘 지내요?**    *Is your younger brother doing well?*    ▸ 은: *Added to letters ending in a consonant.*

- **부모님은 잘 지내세요?**    *Are your parents doing well?*    ▸ *'부모님' requires the honorific ending '-시-'.*
  ▸ 지내(다) + -시- + -어요 → 지내시어요 → 지내세요

## EXPRESSION SKETCHES

*Sibling titles in Korean change depending on the speaker's gender.*

## 2. PARTICLES ①  저는 N을/를 먹어요. I eat N.

# 저는 김치를 먹어요.
**I eat kimchi.**

- The particle '을/를' is attached after the object of the sentence.
- In this sentence, '김치', the object of the verb '먹다', is marked with '을/를'.

## STRUCTURE

**저** + **는** ∨ **김치** + **를** ∨ **먹**(다) + **-어요.**

| [Pronoun] | [Particle] | [Noun] | [Particle] | [Verb] | [Ending] |
|---|---|---|---|---|---|
| The humble form of '나(I)'. | Indicates the topic of the sentence. | Kimchi. | Indicates the object of the sentence. | To eat. | Expresses informal polite style. |

▸ 저는 김치를 먹어요

## MORE EXPRESSIONS

- 저는 **사과**를 먹어요.   *I eat an apple.*

- 저는 **비빔밥**을 먹어요.   *I eat bibimbap.*   ▸ 을: *Added to letters ending in a consonant.*

- 저는 **빵**을 먹어요.   *I eat bread.*

## DIALOG GLIMPSES

유나 씨는 김치를 먹어요?
*Do you eat kimchi, Yuna?*

네, 저는 김치를 먹어요.
*Yes, I eat kimchi.*

**2. PARTICLES ①**   여기는 N이/가 맛있어요.  Here, N is delicious.

# 여기는 커피가 맛있어요.
**Here, the coffee is delicious.**

LISTEN & REPEAT

– The particle '이/가' is attached after the subject of the sentence.
– In this sentence, '여기' is being discussed as a topic, and '커피', the subject of the adjective '맛있다', is marked with '이/가'.

## STRUCTURE

**여기** + **는** ∨ **커피** + **가** ∨ **맛있**(다) + **-어요.**

| | | | | | |
|---|---|---|---|---|---|
| [Pronoun] Here. | [Particle] Indicates the topic of the sentence. | [Noun] Coffee. | [Particle] Indicates the subject of the sentence. | [Adjective] To be delicious. | [Ending] Expresses informal polite style. |

▸ 여기는 커피가 맛있어요

## MORE EXPRESSIONS

– 여기는 **김밥**이 맛있어요.    *Here, the gimbap is delicious.*    ▸ 이: Added to letters ending in a consonant.

– 여기는 **불고기**가 맛있어요.    *Here, the bulgogi is delicious.*

– 여기는 **라면**이 맛있어요.    *Here, the ramyeon is delicious.*    ▸ '라면' is Korean instant noodles.

## EXPRESSION SKETCHES

**커피**

**김밥**

**불고기**

**라면**

## 2. PARTICLES ① 저는 N에 살아요. I live in N.

# 저는 서울에 살아요.
**I live in Seoul.**

LISTEN & REPEAT

- *The particle '에' is attached after the adverbial in a sentence, mainly indicating location and time.*
- *'에' indicates the preceding word is a place with verbs like '살다(to live)' or '있다/없다(to be/to not be)'. Similarly, '에' indicates the direction of movement with verbs like '가다(to go)' or '오다(to come)'.*

## STRUCTURE

**저** + **는** ∨ **서울** + **에** ∨ **살**(다) + **-아요.**

| | | | | | |
|---|---|---|---|---|---|
| *[Pronoun]* | *[Particle]* | *[Noun]* | *[Particle]* | *[Verb]* | *[Ending]* |
| The humble form of '나(I)'. | Indicates the topic of the sentence. | Seoul. | Indicates location. | To live. | Expresses informal polite style. |

▸ 저는 서울에 살아요

## MORE EXPRESSIONS

- 저는 **부산**에 살아요.　　*I live in Busan.*

- 저는 **뉴욕**에 살아요.　　*I live in New York.*

- 저는 **아파트**에 살아요.　*I live in an apartment.*

## EXPRESSIVE TIPS

*In Korean, there are 'case particles' like '이/가', '을/를', and '에' that indicate if the preceding word is the subject, object, adverb, etc., of the sentence. There are also 'auxiliary particles' like '은/는(topic)', '도(too)', and '만(only)' that add special meaning to the preceding word. Therefore, in the sentence '저는 서울에 살아요.', both '는' and '에' are particles, but their usage is different.*
*However, case particles can also function as auxiliary particles, and particles are often left out in everyday conversation. The role of particles in a sentence can be understood based on context or situation. While studying with this textbook, you will come to understand the difference well.*

## 2. PARTICLES ① 저는 N에 운동해요. I work out in N.

# 저는 아침에 운동해요.
**I work out in the morning.**

LISTEN & REPEAT
✓ ☐ ☐ ☐ ☐

- The particle '에' is attached after the adverbial in a sentence, mainly indicating location and time.
- The verb '하다' means 'to do', and is widely used on its own. It also combines with nouns to form various '하다 verbs'. For example, '운동(exercise)' is a noun, and it becomes a verb when '하다' is attached to it.

## STRUCTURE

**저** + **는** ∨ **아침** + **에** ∨ **운동**(하다) + **-해요.**

| [Pronoun] The humble form of '나(I)'. | [Particle] Indicates the topic of the sentence. | [Noun] Morning. | [Particle] Indicates time. | [Verb] To exercise. | [Ending] Expresses informal polite style. |

▸ 저는 아침에 운동해요

## MORE EXPRESSIONS

- **저는 점심에 운동해요.**   *I work out at noon.*

- **저는 저녁에 운동해요.**   *I work out in the evening.*

- **저는 밤에 운동해요.**   *I work out at night.*

## EXPRESSION SKETCHES

**아침**

**점심**

**저녁**

**밤**

## 2. PARTICLES ① 저는 N에서 왔어요. I came from N.

# 저는 미국에서 왔어요.
**I came from the United States.**

- *The particle '에서' is attached after the adverbial in a sentence. It indicates a departure point.*
- *The verb '오다(to come)' is used when talking about one's country or region of origin, as well as when literally coming from a place, as in '저는 집에서 왔어요(I came from home).'*

### STRUCTURE ·······························································

**저** + **는** ∨ **미국** + **에서** ∨ **오(다)** + **-았-** + **-어요.**

| [Pronoun] | [Particle] | [Noun] | [Particle] | [Verb] | [Ending] | [Ending] |
|---|---|---|---|---|---|---|
| The humble form of '나(I)'. | Indicates the topic of the sentence. | The United States. America. | Indicates a departure point or a place. | To come. | Expresses the past tense. | Expresses informal polite style. |

▶ 저는 미국에서 **오았**어요 → 저는 미국에서 **왔**어요

### MORE EXPRESSIONS ·······························································

- 저는 **프랑스**에서 왔어요.   *I came from France.*

- 저는 **브라질**에서 왔어요.   *I came from Brazil.*

- 저는 **일본**에서 왔어요.   *I came from Japan.*

### EXPRESSIVE TIPS

*The particle '에서' is used after a place where an action is taking place, like in '저는 공원에서 운동해요 (I exercise at the park).' or '서울에서 만나요(Let's meet in Seoul).' It shows where activities like exercising or meeting take place.*
*When used with movement verbs like '오다(to come)', '에서' also shows the starting point of an action. It specifies where an action begins. For examples, '저는 서울에서 출발해요(I depart from Seoul).' and '학교에서 집으로 가요(I'm going from school to home).' Here, '에서' marks the starting point of the movement.*

# When and which honorifics should I use?

Korean has many ways to show respect, called honorifics. Here are some key methods:

First, a common way to show respect to **the subject of a sentence** is adding the ending '-시/으시-'.

**동생이 책을 읽어요.** *My younger brother reads a book.*

**선생님께서 책을 읽으세요.** *My teacher reads a book.*

In the first sentence, where the subject 'younger brother' does not need to be elevated, the general subject particle '이/가' is used, followed by '-어요' added to the verb stem '읽'. In the second sentence, where the subject 'teacher' requires respect, a different particle is used, with the honorific ending '-으시-' added between the verb stem '읽' and '-어요'. To show respect for the target of the particle, regardless of the preceding word's form, '께서' is used instead of '이/가', and '께서는' replaces '은/는'.

Sometimes, respect is shown to **the listener** instead of the subject of the sentence. The level of respect is shown by the sentence-closing ending. In this textbook, '-아요/어요/해요' is used for the 'informal polite style,' which is common for general politeness. However, there are many other sentence-closing endings for different levels of formality and respect. The three most common forms are:

① *Informal Casual Style*    ② *Informal Polite Style*    ③ *Formal Polite Style*

**나는 책을 읽어.** / **저는 책을 읽어요.** / **저는 책을 읽습니다.** *I read a book.*

① is called '반말'. This style drops '요', and is used among close acquaintances, known as '말을 놓다(to speak casually)'. Using 반말 with someone you've just met is rude. In this style, humble expressions like '저' are not needed. ② is the most common considered and safe style. It's suitable for many social interactions without offending anyone. ③ used in very respectful contexts, this style is also suitable for everyday conversations with superiors. It uses endings like '-ㅂ니다/습니다' to show high respect.

## 3. MAKING A REQUSET   N 주세요. Please give me N.

# 가방 주세요.
**Please give me the bag.**

- *This is a very common expression used to request something in restaurants, cafes, shops, etc.*
- *In everyday conversation, particles are often left out, so the particle '을/를' after '가방', the object of '주다', is omitted. Subjects or listeners that are obvious are also commonly left out.*

## STRUCTURE

**가방**  ∨  **주**(다)  +  **-시-**  +  **-어요.**

[Noun]
Bag.

[Verb]
To give.

[Ending]
Expresses honorific.

[Ending]
Expresses informal polite style.

▸ 가방(을) 주시어요 → 가방 주세요

## MORE EXPRESSIONS

- **휴대폰 주세요.**   *Please give me your <u>mobile phone</u>.*

  ▸ '핸드폰(*hand phone)' and '휴대 전화('전화' means 'phone'.)' are also common terms for mobile phones.

- **여권 주세요.**   *Please give me your <u>passport</u>.*

- **우산 주세요.**   *Please give me <u>an umbrella</u>.*

## EXPRESSION SKETCHES

**가방**

**휴대폰**

**여권**

**우산**

## 3. MAKING A REQUSET   이거 V-아/어/해 주세요.   Please V this (for me).

# 이거 계산해 주세요.

**Please check this out.**

LISTEN & REPEAT

- *To ask for the bill after buying something or eating, you can use this sentence or simply '계산해 주세요' without '이거'.*
- *'주다' is a verb meaning 'to give', but when used with other verbs in the pattern '-아/어/해 주다', it expresses doing an action for someone else.*

## STRUCTURE

# 이거 ∨ 계산(하다) + -해 주(다) + -시- + -어요.

**[Pronoun]**
*The spoken form of '이것(this thing)'.*

**[Verb]**
*To check out, calculate.*

**[Pattern]**
*Expresses doing an action for someone else.*

**[Ending]**
*Expresses honorific.*

**[Ending]**
*Expresses informal polite style.*

▸ 이거(를) 계산해 주**시어**요 → 이거 계산해 주**세**요

## MORE EXPRESSIONS

– 이거 **교환해** 주세요.   *Please exchange this.*

– 이거 **환불해** 주세요.   *Please refund this.*

– 이거 **깎아** 주세요.   *Please discount this.*   ▸ -아 주다: *Added to letters whose vowel is* ㅏ/ㅗ.

## DIALOG GLIMPSES

**이거 계산해 주세요.**
*Please check this out.*

**네, 주세요.**
*Yes, please give it to me.*

## 3. MAKING A REQUSET  안 Adv 해 주세요. Please make it not Adv.

# 안 맵게 해 주세요.

**Please make it not spicy.**

LISTEN & REPEAT

- *You can use this expression to tell restaurants your food preferences in advance.*
- *The verb '하다(to do)' has many uses, so the sentence literally means to 'Please do it not spicy.'*

## STRUCTURE

# 안 ∨ 맵게 + 해 주(다) + -시- + -어요.

| | | | | |
|---|---|---|---|---|
| *[Adverb]* | *[Adverb]* | *[Pattern]* | *[Ending]* | *[Ending]* |
| Not. | Spicily. | Expresses doing an action for someone else. | Expresses honorific. | Expresses informal polite style. |

▸ 안 맵게 해 주**시어**요 → 안 맵게 해 주**세**요

## MORE EXPRESSIONS

- 안 **짜게** 해 주세요.　　*Please make it not salty.*

- 안 **달게** 해 주세요.　　*Please make it not sweet.*

- 안 **아프게** 해 주세요.　*Please make it not painful.*

## EXPRESSIVE TIPS

*By attaching the ending '-게' to the stem of adjectives, they are transformed into adverbs. The words mentioned above are conjugated by attaching '-게' to '맵다(to be spicy)', '짜다(to be salty)', '달다(to be sweet)', and '아프다(to be painful)'.*

*The word '맛있게' in the previously learned sentence '맛있게 드세요(Enjoy your meal).' is also used as an adverb, formed by attaching '-게' to the stem of the adjective '맛있다(to be delicious)'. The direct translation of the sentence is "Please eat deliciously."*

**3. MAKING A REQUSET**  N 넣어/빼 주시겠어요? Would you add/take out N, please?

# 설탕 넣어 주시겠어요?

**Would you add sugar, please?**

LISTEN & REPEAT

- *You can use this in a cafe or restaurant to ask to add or remove an ingredient from your food.*
- *The ending '-겠-' not only expresses the subject's will but is also used to indicate a polite or indirect manner of speaking.*

## STRUCTURE

설탕 ∨ 넣(다) + -어 주(다) + -시- + -겠- + -어요?

| [Noun] Sugar. | [Verb] To put in. | [Pattern] Expresses doing an action for someone else. | [Ending] Expresses honorific. | [Ending] Expresses subject's will. | [Ending] Expresses informal polite style. |

▸ 설탕(을) 넣어 주시겠어요 → 설탕 넣어 주시겠어요

## MORE EXPRESSIONS

- **소금** 넣어 주시겠어요?   *Would you add salt, please?*

- **시럽** 빼 주시겠어요?   *Would you take out the syrup, please?*   ▸ '빼다' means 'to leave out'.

- **견과류** 빼 주시겠어요?   *Would you take out the nuts, please?*

## EXPRESSION SKETCHES

설탕을 넣어요.

소금을 넣어요.

시럽을 빼요.

견과류를 빼요.

**3. MAKING A REQUSET** N 좀 (V) 주실 수 있으세요? Could you V N, please?

# 반찬 좀 더 주실 수 있으세요?

**Could you give me some more side dishes, please?**

LISTEN & REPEAT
☑ ☐ ☐ ☐

- *The pattern '-ㄹ/을 수 있(다)' expresses the ability to perform a task or the possibility of a state.*
- *Using this form to ask someone if they can do something is a very polite way to ask.*
- *For your information, refilling side dishes is usually free in most restaurants, so it's good to ask first.*

## STRUCTURE

# 좀 ∨ 더 ∨ 주(다) + -시- + -ㄹ 수 있(다) + -으시- + -어요?

| [Adverb] | [Adverb] | [Verb] | [Ending] | [Pattern] | [Ending] | [Ending] |
|---|---|---|---|---|---|---|
| A little. | More. | To give. | Expresses honorific. | Expresses the ability to do something. | Expresses honorific. | Expresses informal polite style. |

▸ 반찬(을) 좀 더 주**시ㄹ** 수 있으**시어**요 → 반찬 좀 더 주**실** 수 있으**세**요

## MORE EXPRESSIONS

– **길** 좀 **알려** 주실 수 있으세요?    *Could you tell me the way, please?*

– **여기** 좀 **닦아** 주실 수 있으세요?    *Could you clean this up, please?*

– **저** 좀 **도와**주실 수 있으세요?    *Could you help me, please?*

▸ *In some cases, the pattern 'V-아/어/해 주다', which means to do V for someone else, has become fixed, it is written as one word without spaces, such as '도와주다'.*

## EXPRESSIVE TIPS

*The adverb '좀' is a shortened form of '조금(a little)', and it's often used to make requests sound softer. For example, '길 좀 알려 주세요.' sounds much softer and less direct than '길 알려 주세요.' It's similar to the difference between 'Could you tell me the way?' and 'Tell me the way.' While '길 알려 주세요.' is not rude, it can seem more assertive, like you are demanding something obvious.*

# 제가 도와드릴까요?

**May I help you?**

LISTEN & REPEAT
✓ ☐ ☐ ☐

- *The ending '-ㄹ/을까' is used to ask for the listener's intent.*
- *'드리다' is the honorific of '주다'. Therefore, it is also used in the pattern '-아/어/해 드리다' like '-아/어/해 주다'. When helping 'me', you use '도와주다', but when helping 'someone else', you use '도와드리다' to show respect.*

## STRUCTURE

**제** + **가** ∨ **도와드리**(다) + **-ㄹ까** + **요?**

*[Pronoun]*
*The form of '저(I)' when the particle '가' is attached.*

*[Particle]*
*Indicates the subject of the sentence.*

*[Verb]*
*The honorific of '도와주다(to help out)'.*

*[Ending]*
*Expresses asking for the listener's intent.*

*Indicates respect to the listener.*

▸ 제가 도와드리**ㄹ**까요 → 제가 도와드릴까요

## MORE EXPRESSIONS

- 제가 **빌려**드릴까요?   *May I lend it to you?*

- 제가 **잡아** 드릴까요?   *May I hold it for you?*

- 제가 **꺼내** 드릴까요?   *May I take it out for you?*

▸ *The sentences on this page are commonly used even without '제가'.*

▸ *-어 주다(드리다): Added to letters whose vowel is not ㅏ/ㅗ.*
▸ 꺼내(다) + -어 주다 → 꺼내어 주다 → 꺼내 주다

## DIALOG GLIMPSES

**제가 도와드릴까요?**
*May I help you?*

**아니요, 괜찮아요.**
*No, it's fine.*

**3. MAKING A REQUSET**   저희 같이 V-아/어/해요. Let's V together.

# 저희 같이 구경해요.
**Let's look around together.**

- *Stating the predicate alone can sound a command or suggestion; adding '저희' makes it a request.*
- *In Korean, you can elevate the listener not just with direct honorifics but also by lowering yourself, which indirectly raises the listener's status. This is shown with humble forms like '저' and '저희'.*

## STRUCTURE

**저희**  ∨  **같이**  ∨  **구경**(하다)  +  **-해요.**

[Pronoun]
The humble form of
'우리(we)'.

[Adverb]
Together.

[Verb]
To look around.

[Ending]
Expresses
informal polite style.

▸ 저희 같이 구경해요

## MORE EXPRESSIONS

– 저희 같이 **산책해**요.   Let's *take a walk* together.   ▸ It can also be used without
'같이(together)'.

– 저희 같이 **들어가**요.   Let's *go inside* together.   ▸ -아요: Added to letters whose vowel is
ㅏ/ㅗ.
▸ 들어가(다) + -아요 → 들어가아요 → 들어가요.

– 저희 같이 **나가**요.   Let's *go out* together.

## DIALOG GLIMPSES

**저희 같이 구경해요.**
*Let's look around together.*

**그래요.**
*OK.*

# 아무거나 시켜도 돼요?

**Is it okay if I order anything?**

LISTEN & REPEAT
✓ □ □ □

- *The pattern '-아/어/해도 되다' expresses permission or allowance for an action.*
- *The particle '나' indicates that any choice is acceptable among several options.*
- *'아무' refers to any person or thing without specifying, and it is not used alone.*

## STRUCTURE

**아무거** + **나** ∨ **시키**(다) + **-어도 되**(다) + **-어요?**

| [Pronoun] | [Particle] | [Verb] | [Pattern] | [Ending] |
|---|---|---|---|---|
| *The spoken form of '아무것(anything)'.* | *Indicates that any choice is acceptable.* | *To order.* | *Expresses permission or allowance for an action.* | *Expresses informal polite style.* |

▸ 아무거나 시**키어**도 **되어**요 → 아무거나 시**켜**도 **돼**요

## MORE EXPRESSIONS

- **아무나 불러도 돼요?**  *Is it okay if I call anyone?*

- **아무 데나 앉아도 돼요?**  *Is it okay if I sit anywhere?*

- **아무렇게나 해도 돼요?**  *Is it okay if I do it any way I want?*

▸ *Don't memorize '아무' and the particle '나' separately, but remember them together as '아무나(anyone)', '아무 데나 (anywhere)', '아무렇게나(anyhow)'.*

## DIALOG GLIMPSES

**아무거나 시켜도 돼요?**
*Is it okay if I order anything?*

**안 돼요.**
*No.*

# Why do Koreans speak without the particle?

*One of the main functions of particles is to attach to the end of a word in a sentence, indicating the role of that word.*

*subject particle '가'*

**민서가 커피를 마셔요.** *Minseo drinks coffee.*

*object particle '를'*

*Here, the subject particle '가' and the object particle '를' show that '민서' is the subject and '커피' is the object of the sentence. However, particles are often left out in actual conversation.*

*There are no strict rules for omitting particles. They are almost always omitted in very casual conversations, and it's safe to assume that particles are not left out depending on the context. The extent of omission varies depending on the speaking situation, the relationship with the listener, and if the speaker wants to emphasize certain words.*

*① Complete sentence*        *② Omission of particles*        *③ Omission of an obvious subject*

**저는 가방이 있어요.**  >  **저 가방 있어요.**  >  **가방 있어요.** *I have a bag.*

*In everyday conversation, responses like ② or ③ are common when asked if you have a bag. Using all particles as in ① can feel unnatural.*
*Keeping particles can intentionally add special meaning. For example, to emphasize that others might not have it, but 'I' do, one might say, "**저는 가방 있어요.**" Or to highlight 'the bag', you could say, "**저 가방이 있어요.**"*

*Understanding the common omission of particles in everyday Korean conversation will help you understand and speak more naturally.*

## 4. NUMBERS

# 1(일)부터 10(십)까지

**From one to ten (Sino-Korean numbers)**

LISTEN & REPEAT
✓ ☐ ☐ ☐ ☐

– In Korean, there are two number systems. One of them, the Sino-Korean numbers, is commonly used in various situations; for money, telephone numbers and addresses, bus numbers, minutes/seconds (on a clock), years/ months/days (on a calendar), and for measurements such as height and weight.

SINO-KOREAN NUMBERS ·······································································

| 일 | 이 | 삼 | 사 | 오 | 육 | 칠 | 팔 | 구 | 십 |
|---|---|---|---|---|---|---|---|---|---|
| 1 | 2 | 3 | 4 | 5 | 6 | 7 | 8 | 9 | 10 |

| 십일 | 십이 | 십삼 | 십사 | 십오 | 십육 | 십칠 | 십팔 | 십구 | 이십 |
|---|---|---|---|---|---|---|---|---|---|
| 11 | 12 | 13 | 14 | 15 | 16 | 17 | 18 | 19 | 20 |

| 이십일 | 이십이 | 이십삼 | 이십사 | 이십오 | 이십육 | 이십칠 | 이십팔 | 이십구 | 삼십 |
|---|---|---|---|---|---|---|---|---|---|
| 21 | 22 | 23 | 24 | 25 | 26 | 27 | 28 | 29 | 30 |

| 사십 | 오십 | 육십 | 칠십 | 팔십 | 구십 | 백 | 천 | 만 | 영/공 |
|---|---|---|---|---|---|---|---|---|---|
| 40 | 50 | 60 | 70 | 80 | 90 | 100 | 1,000 | 10,000 | 0 |

HOW TO READ

- Numbers are read digit by digit, from left to right.
- Use terms like '십(10)/백(100)/천(1,000)/만(10,000)' for each digit's position, placing the number before these terms.
- For two or more digits, '1(일)' can be omitted.
  For example, 1,000 is more commonly read as 천 rather than 일천.
- For instance, '365' is read as '삼백(300), 육십(60), 오(5)', and '10,510' is read as '만(10,000), 오백(500), 십(10)'.

# 하나부터 열까지

## From one to ten (Native Korean numbers)

LISTEN & REPEAT

☑ ☐ ☐ ☐

– *The other system, the native Korean numbers, is primarily used for counting objects along with unit nouns. It is also used to express age and hours (on a clock). This numbering system is used when counting down from three to one in front of a camera, or saying 'Come here while I count to three(셋).'*

### NATIVE KOREAN NUMBERS

| 하나 | 둘 | 셋 | 넷 | 다섯 | 여섯 | 일곱 | 여덟 | 아홉 | 열 |
|---|---|---|---|---|---|---|---|---|---|
| 1 | 2 | 3 | 4 | 5 | 6 | 7 | 8 | 9 | 10 |

| 열하나 | 열둘 | 열셋 | 열넷 | 열다섯 | 열여섯 | 열일곱 | 열여덟 | 열아홉 | 스물 |
|---|---|---|---|---|---|---|---|---|---|
| 11 | 12 | 13 | 14 | 15 | 16 | 17 | 18 | 19 | 20 |

| 스물하나 | 스물둘 | 스물셋 | 스물넷 | 스물다섯 | 스물여섯 | 스물일곱 | 스물여덟 | 스물아홉 | 서른 |
|---|---|---|---|---|---|---|---|---|---|
| 21 | 22 | 23 | 24 | 25 | 26 | 27 | 28 | 29 | 30 |

| 마흔 | 쉰 | 예순 | 일흔 | 여든 | 아흔 | 백 |
|---|---|---|---|---|---|---|
| 40 | 50 | 60 | 70 | 80 | 90 | 100 |

### HOW TO READ

- *The method of reading is basically the same as with Sino-Korean numbers. However, this number system has special names for numbers like 20, 30, 40, 50, 60, 70, 80, 90.*
- *Numbers that exceed three digits are almost never read in this number system.*
- *There are numbers that change form when combined with unit nouns.*
  *These include '1(하나 → 한)', '2(둘 → 두)', '3(셋 → 세)', '4(넷 → 네)', '20(스물 → 스무)'.*
- *For instance, '34' is read as '서른(30), 넷(4)', and when used with the unit noun for counting age '살', it is read as '서른네 살', not '서른넷 살'.*

# 달력 보기 (년/월/일)

## Reading a calendar (year/month/day)

LISTEN & REPEAT

## 2034년 이천삼십사 년 / 5월 오월

| Sunday<br>일요일 | Monday<br>월요일 | Tuesday<br>화요일 | Wednesday<br>수요일 | Thursday<br>목요일 | Friday<br>금요일 | Saturday<br>토요일 |
|---|---|---|---|---|---|---|
| | 1<br>일 일 | 2<br>이 일 | 3<br>삼 일 | 4<br>사 일 | 5<br>오 일 | 6<br>육 일 |
| 7<br>칠 일 | 8<br>팔 일 | 9<br>구 일 | 10<br>십 일 | 11<br>십일 일 | 12<br>십이 일 | 13<br>십삼 일 |
| 14<br>십사 일 | 15<br>십오 일 | 16<br>십육 일 | 17<br>십칠 일 | 18<br>십팔 일 | 19<br>십구 일 | 20<br>이십 일 |
| 21<br>이십일 일 | 22<br>이십이 일 | 23<br>이십삼 일 | 24<br>이십사 일 | 25<br>이십오 일 | 26<br>이십육 일 | 27<br>이십칠 일 |
| 28<br>이십팔 일 | 29<br>이십구 일 | 30<br>삼십 일 | 31<br>삼십일 일 | | | |

## HOW TO READ

- The year(년), month(월), and day(일) on calendars are read using the Sino-Korean number system.

- Exceptions in spelling or pronunciation are as follows.
  - 6월: 유월, not 육월.
  - 10월: 시월, not 십월.
  - 16일: [심뉴길], not [시뷰길].
  - 26일: [이심뉴길], not [이시뷰길]

- Let's read the dates displayed on the calendar.
  - A: 몇 년이에요(What year is it)?
    B: 이천삼십사 년이에요.
  - A: 몇 월이에요(What month is it)?
    B: 오월이에요.
  - A: 며칠이에요(What date is it)?
    B: 이십사 일이에요.
  - A: 무슨 요일이에요
    (What day of the week is it)?
    B: 금요일이에요.

- Related vocabulary
  - 그저께: 2 days ago
  - 어제: yesterday
  - 오늘: today
  - 내일: tomorrow
  - 내일모레: 2 days later

# 시계 보기 (시/분/초)

**Reading a clock (hour/minute/second)**

LISTEN & REPEAT

A: 지금 몇 시예요(*What time is it now*)?
B: 열 시 이십오 분이에요(*It's ten twenty-five*).
A: 몇 초예요(*What second*)?
B: 사십 초예요(*It's forty seconds*).

## HOW TO READ

- Hours(시) are read using native Korean numbers, while minutes(분), seconds(초) are read using Sino-Korean numbers. For example, it's '여덟(8) 시 오십(50) 분 칠(7) 초'.
- When it's exactly on the hour, you simply say '시', like "여덟 시예요(*It's eight*)."

- Times can also be read in a different way.

| 2:00 | 5:30 | 3:50 | 3:55 |
|------|------|------|------|
| 두 시 | 다섯 시 삼십 분 | 세 시 오십 분 | 세 시 오십오 분 |
| = 두 시 정각 | = 다섯 시 반 | = 네 시 십 분 전 | = 네 시 오 분 전 |
| (*Two o'clock*) | (*Half past five*) | (*Ten minutes to four*) | (*Five minutes to four*) |

- Related vocabulary
  - 오전: *A.M.*
  - 오후: *P.M.*

# 단위 명사

**Unit nouns**

LISTEN & REPEAT
☑ ☐ ☐ ☐

– *When counting the number of objects, you can simply use native Korean numbers (e.g., '사과 하나'). But you can also uses unit nouns(counter words) to specify the quantities. There are various unit nouns depending on the object.*

## UNIT NOUNS

○ **개**
For individual items.

사과 한 개
*1 apple*

사과 열 개
*10 apples*

○ **잔**
For cups or glasses of drinks or alcohol.

커피 두 잔
*2 cups of coffee*

커피 스물한 잔
*21 cups of coffee*

○ **병**
For bottles of liquids or powders.

맥주 세 병
*3 bottles of beer*

맥주 스물두 병
*22 bottles of beer*

○ **권**
For books.

책 네 권
*4 books*

책 스물네 권
*24 books*

○ **명**
For people.

여자 다섯 명
*5 women*

여자 스물다섯 명
*25 women*

○ **분**
For people, used respectfully.

할머니 열 분
*10 elderly women*

할머니 서른 분
*30 eldely women*

○ **마리**
For animals, fish, insects, etc.

고양이 열한 마리
*11 cats*

고양이 백 마리
*100 cats*

## HOW TO READ

- *As learned in the number units previously, most unit nouns are read with native Korean numbers, and there are numbers that change form when directly combined with unit nouns(하나, 둘, 셋, 넷, 스물).*
- *However, Sino-Korean numbers are sometimes used with unit nouns, such as 'cm(length), kg(weight), 동(building), 호(room numbers), 원(price)', in contexts like measurements and calculations even though there isn't a strict standard for this.*

## KOREAN NATIVE VIBE TIPS
일 이 삼 *vs.* 하나 둘 셋

# Sino-Korean Numbers

*Dates*
*2024. 3. 27.*
**이천이십사 년 삼월 이십칠 일**

*Time (minutes, seconds)*
*1:35:15*
**삼십오 분 십오 초**

*Money*
*23,000 won*
**이만삼천 원**

*Building*
*Building 2 / 23rd floor / Room 2013*
**이 동 / 이십삼 층 / 이천십삼 호**

*Telephone*
*010-1234-5678*
**공일공 일이삼사 에(-) 오육칠팔**

*Bus*
*3421*
**삼사이일 / 삼천사백이십일**

*Some Unit Nouns*
*미터(m), 그램(g), 퍼센트(%), etc.*
**일 그램**

*Unit Nouns (large quantities)*
*314 balls*
**공 삼백십사 개**

# Native Korean Numbers

*Age*
*31 years old*
**서른하나 / 서른한 살**

*Time (hours)*
*1:00*
**한 시**

*Countdown*
*3 2 1*
**셋 둘 하나**

*Counting in Order*
*1 2 3*
**하나 둘 셋**

*The Number of Objects*
*2 kids*
**두 아이**

*The Number of Repetitions*
*4 times*
**네 번**

*Some Unit Nouns*
*개, 잔, 병, 권, 장, 대, etc.*
**한 잔**

*Unit Nouns (small quantities)*
*14 balls*
**공 열네 개**

## 5. ASKING QUESTIONS 뭐 V-아/어/해요? What are you V?

# 뭐 해요?

**What are you doing?**

LISTEN & REPEAT
✓ ☐ ☐ ☐

- It's a casual expression to ask what someone is doing. Sometimes the simple present tense in its basic form can mean the present continuous tense.
- If you need to be more respectful, you would ask, '뭐 하세요?' which includes the honorific ending '-시-'.

## STRUCTURE

| 뭐 | ∨ | (하다) | + | -해요? |

**[Pronoun]**
Referring to an unknown fact or object. What.

**[Verb]**
To do.

**[Ending]**
Expresses informal polite style.

▸ 뭐(를) 해요 → 뭐 해요

## MORE EXPRESSIONS

– **뭐 먹어요?**   *What are you eating?*   ▸ -어요: Added to letters whose vowel is not ㅏ/ㅗ.

– **뭐 마셔요?**   *What are you drinking?*   ▸ 마시(다) + -어요 → 마시어요 → 마셔요

– **뭐 봐요?**   *What are you watching?*   ▸ 보(다) + -아요 → 보아요 → 봐요

## EXPRESSION SKETCHES

**해요.**

**먹어요.**

**마셔요.**

**봐요.**

# 여기 뭐가 맛있어요?

**What's delicious here?**

LISTEN & REPEAT

– *You can say this when you're at a restaurant or cafe and can't decide what to order.*
– *It's about selecting or identifying something specific from a range of options, so the particle '가' is used to highlight the subject of the question.*

## STRUCTURE

**여기** ∨ **뭐** + **가** ∨ **맛있**(다) + **-어요?**

[Pronoun]
*Referring to a place close to the speaker. Here.*

[Pronoun]
*Referring to an unknown fact or object. What.*

[Particle]
*Indicates the subject of the sentence.*

[Adjective]
*To be delicious.*

[Ending]
*Expresses informal polite style.*

▸ 여기(**는**) 뭐가 맛있어요 → 여기 뭐가 맛있어요

## MORE EXPRESSIONS

– 여기 뭐가 **잘 나가**요?     *What's popular here?*     ▸ *The verb '나가다(to go out)' also used to mean 'to sell well' or 'to be popular'.*

– 여기 뭐가 **들어 있**어요?     *What's in here?*

– 여기 뭐가 **어울려**요?     *What suits here?*

## DIALOG GLIMPSES

**여기 뭐가 맛있어요?**
*What's delicious here?*

**아이스 라테가 잘 나가요.**
*The iced latte is very popular.*

# 이거 얼마예요?

**How much is this?**

LISTEN & REPEAT

– You can use this expression to ask about the price of something.
– '이거/저거/그거(this/that/the thing)' are demonstrative pronouns that refer to objects based on the speaker and listener's positions, respectively referred to in written language as '이것/저것/그것.'

## STRUCTURE

| 이거 | ∨ | 얼마 | + | 이(다) | + | -에요? |
|---|---|---|---|---|---|---|

**[Pronoun]**
The spoken form
of '이것(this thing).'

**[Noun]**
A quantity or degree
that you do not know.
How much.

Attached after a noun
to describe it.

**[Ending]**
Expresses
informal polite style.

▸ 이거(는) 얼마**이에**요 → 이거 얼마**예**요

## MORE EXPRESSIONS

– **저거** 얼마예요?  How much is <u>that thing</u>?

▸ 저거: Referring to things far from both the speaker and the listener.

– **그거** 얼마예요?  How much is <u>the thing</u>?

▸ 그거: Referring to things far from the speaker but close to the listener, or to a subject already mentioned earlier.

– 얼마예요?  How much is it?

## EXPRESSION SKETCHES

이거

그거

저거

# 언제 가요?

**When are you going?**

LISTEN & REPEAT

– *You can use this expression to ask when to do a certain action.*
– *When the subject is omitted, you can understand what it refers to from the context. Even if it's not 'you', it can be omitted if both the speaker and the listener know what's being discussed.*

## STRUCTURE

**언제**  ∨  **가(다)**  +  **-아요?**

[Pronoun]
*Referring to a time when one is unsure. When.*

[Verb]
*To go.*

[Ending]
*Expresses informal polite style.*

▸ 언제 **가아**요 → 언제 **가**요

## MORE EXPRESSIONS

– 언제 **시작해**요?  *When does it start?*

– 언제 **끝나**요?  *When does it end?*

– 언제 **출발해**요?  *When does it leave?*

## DIALOG GLIMPSES

**우리 언제 가요?**
*When are we going?*

**음, 저녁에 갈까요?**
*Hmm, shall we go in the evening?*

# 버스 언제 와요?

**When does the bus come?**

LISTEN & REPEAT

– When you're curious about when something will arrive, you can use this expression. Start by mentioning what you're curious about.

– You can usually find out when the bus is coming through the electronic display at the bus stop or via an app.

## STRUCTURE

**버스** ∨ **언제** ∨ **오**(다) + -**아요?**

*[Noun]*
Bus.

*[Pronoun]*
Referring to a time when one is unsure. When.

*[Verb]*
To come.

*[Ending]*
Expresses informal polite style.

▸ 버스(<u>는</u>) 언제 **오아**요 → 버스 언제 **와**요

## MORE EXPRESSIONS

– **지하철** 언제 와요?   *When does the subway come?*

– **택시** 언제 와요?   *When does the taxi come?*

– **배달** 언제 와요?   *When does the delivery come?*

## DIALOG GLIMPSES

버스 언제 와요?
*When does the bus come?*

10분 안에 와요.
*It comes in 10 minutes.*

# 여기가 어디예요?

**Where is this place?**

– *You can use this expression to ask where a certain place is located.*
– *'여기/저기/거기(this/that/the place)' are demonstrative pronouns indicating location based on the speaker and listener's positions, respectively referred to in written language as '이곳/저곳/그곳.'*

## STRUCTURE

**여기** + **가** ∨ **어디** + **이**(다) + **-에요?**

[Pronoun]
*Referring to a place close to the speaker. Here.*

[Particle]
*Indicates the subject of the sentence.*

[Pronoun]
*Referring to an unknown place. Where.*

*Attached after a noun to describe it.*

[Ending]
*Expresses informal polite style.*

▸ 여기가 어디**이에**요 → 여기가 어디**예**요

## MORE EXPRESSIONS

– **저기**가 어디예요?    *Where is that place?*

▸ 저기: *Referring to a place far from both the speaker and the listener.*

– **거기**가 어디예요?    *Where is the place?*

▸ 거기: *Referring to a place far from the speaker but close to the listener, or to a place already mentioned earlier.*

– 어디예요?    *Where is it?*

## EXPRESSION SKETCHES

**여기**

**거기**

**저기**

# 화장실은 어디에 있어요?

**Where is the toilet (located)?**

LISTEN & REPEAT

- *You can use this expression to ask where exactly something is located.*
- *This can be shortened to '화장실 어디 있어요?', and further shortened to '화장실 어딨어요?'*
- *Using the expressions just learned before, '화장실은 어디예요?'*

## STRUCTURE

화장실 + 은 ˅ 어디 + 에 ˅ 있(다) + -어요?

| [Noun] Toilet. Restroom. | [Particle] Indicates the topic of the sentence. | [Pronoun] Referring to an unknown place. Where. | [Particle] Indicates location. | [Adjective] To be/exist. | [Ending] Expresses informal polite style. |

▶ 화장실은 어디에 있어요

## MORE EXPRESSIONS

- **약국**은 어디에 있어요?　　*Where is the pharmacy (located)?*

- **편의점**은 어디에 있어요?　　*Where is the convenience store (located)?*

- **도서관**은 어디에 있어요?　　*Where is the library (located)?*

## EXPRESSION SKETCHES

**화장실**

**약국**

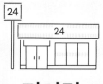

**편의점**

**도서관**

# 주문은 어디에서 해요?

**Where can I place an order?**

LISTEN & REPEAT

– *You can use this expression to ask where an action takes place.*
– *You can also ask like '어디에서 주문해요?'. The verb '주문하다' means 'to order'.*
– *In everyday conversation, '에서' is commonly shortened to '서', as in '어디서'.*

## STRUCTURE

**주문** + **은** ∨ **어디** + **에서** ∨ **(하다)** + **-해요?**

| | | | | | |
|---|---|---|---|---|---|
| [Noun] | [Particle] | [Pronoun] | [Particle] | [Verb] | [Ending] |
| Order. | Indicates the topic of the sentence. | Referring to an unknown place. Where. | Indicates a place. | To do. | Expresses informal polite style. |

▸ 주문은 어디에서 해요

## MORE EXPRESSIONS

– **빨래**는 어디에서 **해**요?   *Where can I do the laundry?*

– **물**은 어디에서 **사**요?   *Where can I buy water?*

– **버스**는 어디에서 **타**요?   *Where can I take the bus?*

## EXPRESSIVE TIPS

*While '주문을 어디에서 해요?' is grammatically accurate, with '을' as the object particle following the noun, it can sound formal or unnatural in casual conversation.*
*Instead, using '은/는' as a topic particle, as in '주문은 어디에서 해요?', emphasizes the topic '주문' and shows the speaker's interest in the action of ordering, making it feel more natural and conversational.*

# 택배는 어떻게 보내요?

**How can I send a package?**

LISTEN & REPEAT
✓ ☐ ☐ ☐

- '어떻게' means 'by what means or method,' and is an adverb used to ask about the manner, means, or process by which a specific action or situation is carried out.
- The '은/는' used after '택배' here, likewise, replaces '을/를' as explained on the previous page.

STRUCTURE ...........................................................................

**택배** + **는** ∨ **어떻게** ∨ **보내**(다) + **-어요?**

| | | | | |
|---|---|---|---|---|
| *[Noun]* | *[Particle]* | *[Adverb]* | *[Verb]* | *[Ending]* |
| *Parcel delivery.* | *Indicates the topic of the sentence.* | *By what means or method. How.* | *To send.* | *Expresses informal polite style.* |

▸ 택배는 어떻게 보**내어**요 → 택배는 어떻게 보**내**요

MORE EXPRESSIONS ...............................................................

- **쓰레기**는 어떻게 **버려**요?  *How can I throw the trash away?*

- **이 문**은 어떻게 **열**어요?  *How can I open this door?*

- **이 창문**은 어떻게 **닫**아요?  *How can I close this window?*

EXPRESSION SKETCHES

택배를 보내요.

쓰레기를 버려요.

문을 열어요.

창문을 닫아요.

# 왜 그래요?

**Why are you like that?**

LISTEN & REPEAT

- '그래' *is a shortened form of* '그리하여', *meaning 'in that way', so the sentence literally means, 'Why do you act in that way?'*
- *Depending on the way you speak, it may sound like you're saying 'What's wrong with you?'*

## STRUCTURE

### 왜    ∨    그래    +    요?

**[Adverb]**
*For what reason.*
*Why.*

*A shortened form of*
'그리하여'*(in that way).*

*Indicates respect*
*to the listener.*

▸ 왜 그래요

## MORE EXPRESSIONS

– **왜 이래**요?   *Why are you* <u>like this</u>?

– **왜 저래**요?   *Why are they* <u>like that</u>?

– 왜요?   *Why?*

▸ *Because the subjects are not explicitly stated in these sentences, they can be freely used in context.*

## DIALOG GLIMPSES

**왜 그래요?**
*Why are you like that?*

**김치가 너무 매워서요.**
*Because the kimchi is too spicy.*

# 이분은 누구세요?

**Who is this person?**

LISTEN & REPEAT ✓ ☐ ☐ ☐

- This is an expression that politely asks who this person is. You can say '이 사람은 누구예요?' without the ending '-시-'.
- '이분/저분/그분(this/that/the person)' are demonstrative pronouns indicating based on the speaker and listener's positions.

## STRUCTURE

**이분** + **은** ∨ **누구** + **-시-** + **-어요?**

| | | | | |
|---|---|---|---|---|
| [Pronoun] | [Particle] | [Pronoun] | [Ending] | [Ending] |
| A honorific of '이 사람(this person)'. | Indicates the topic of the sentence. | Referring to a person you don't know. Who. | Expresses honorific. | Expresses informal polite style. |

▸ 이분은 누구**시어**요 → 이분은 누구**세**요

## MORE EXPRESSIONS

- **저분**은 누구세요?　　*Who is that person?*　　▸ 저분: A honorific of '저 사람(that person)'.

- **그분**은 누구세요?　　*Who is the person?*　　▸ 그거: A honorific of '그 사람(the person)'.

- 누구세요?　　　　　　*Who is it?/Who are you?*　　▸ You can use this sentence when a stranger knocks on your door or calls you on the phone.

## EXPRESSION SKETCHES

**이분**

**그분**

**저분**

# 누가 제일 잘해요?

**Who is the best?**

LISTEN & REPEAT

☑ ☐ ☐ ☐

- *You can say this when asking which person is the best in a certain part among others.*
- *When the particle '가' comes right after '누구(who)', it is not said as '누구가' but as '누가'.*

**STRUCTURE** · · · · · · · · · · · · · · · · · · · · · · · · · · · · · · · · · · · · · · · · · · · · · · · · · · · · · · · · · · · · · · ·

**누가**  ∨  **제일**  ∨  **잘**(하다)  +  **-해요?**

*A shortened form of '누구+가(who is)'.*

**[Adverb]**
*Among many, the most.*

**[Adjective]**
*To do something well.*

**[Ending]**
*Expresses informal polite style.*

▸ 누가 제일 잘해요

**MORE EXPRESSIONS** · · · · · · · · · · · · · · · · · · · · · · · · · · · · · · · · · · · · · · · · · · · · · · · · · · · · · ·

- **누가 제일 귀여워요?**  *Who is the cutest?*  ▸ 귀엽(다) + -어요 → 귀여우- + -어요 → 귀여우어요 → 귀여워요 *(Refer to rule number 6 on page 63.)*

- **누가 제일 재미있어요?**  *Who is the most fun?*

- **누가 제일 예뻐요?**  *Who is the prettiest?*

**EXPRESSIVE TIPS**

*In Korean, there are no separate comparative or superlative forms for verbs or adjectives. Instead, adverbs are used in front of them to convey those meanings. The most commonly used words are '더(more)', '덜(less)', and for the superlative, '제일/가장(the most)' are used. Examples of using these adverbs are as follows.*

**'제가 더 예뻐요**(I'm prettier).**', '제가 덜 예뻐요**(I'm less pretty).**', '제가 제일/가장 예뻐요**(I'm the prettiest).**'**

# It seems 은/는 goes beyond marking just the topic of a sentence.

*In real-life Korean conversations, particles are often omitted, and they are used for more than just indicating the role of words in a sentence. Indeed, particles can add special meaning and change the nuance of a sentence. Let's first understand the special auxiliary meaning of '은/는'.*

*The particle '은/는' indicates the topic of a sentence, like "저는 마이클이에요." Because it's so fundamental, it's frequently omitted. Therefore, if '은/는' is not omitted in a sentence, it can be thought to add a special meaning beyond just indicating the topic. A typical auxiliary meaning of '은/는' is to show contrast with something else. A few examples can make this clearer.*

**저는 라면을 먹어요. 하지만 김치는 안 먹어요.** *I eat ramyeon. But I don't eat kimchi.*

*In the second sentence, '김치', which is the object of '먹다', usually would be followed by the object particle '를'. However, '는' is used to highlight a contrast: unlike eating ramyeon, one does not eat kimchi. A Korean would say, "저는 라면을 먹어요. 하지만 김치는 안 먹어요." instead of, "저는 라면을 먹어요. 하지만 김치를 안 먹어요." So if someone says "저는 김치는 안 먹어요." without any context, it means 'I eat other things, but not kimchi'.*

**A: 설탕 있어요?** *Do you have sugar?*          **B: 시럽은 있어요.** *I have syrup.*

*In this case as well, since '이/가' usually comes before '있다/없다(to be/to not be)', you would expect to say "시럽이 있어요." However, '은' is used to better show that, unlike sugar, syrup is available. Hearing this response, even though it doesn't directly say "There is no sugar.", using '은' makes it clear that sugar isn't available, but syrup is.*

*In response to B, A might say, "그럼 시럽 주세요(Then give me syrup).", but could also say, "아, 저는 시럽은 안 먹어요(Ah, I don't eat syrup)." This means 'I don't need syrup because I eat sugar, but not syrup.' Or, in response to A's question, B might say, "설탕은 없어요(I don't have sugar)." This implies that while there is no sugar, something else is available.*

*In all these sentences, while all particles can be omitted, and using '이/가' or '을/를' wouldn't be grammatically wrong, using '은/는' to show contrast is the most natural in these contexts.*

## 6. RESPONSES

# 네.

**Yes.**

- *This is the word most commonly used to respond to a call or to answer yes to a question.*
- *'예' is also used in the same way as '네'. It feels a bit more formal, but it is also common in everyday situations. Both are polite expressions.*

## STRUCTURE

# 네.

*[Exclamation]*
*Yes.*

▸ 네

## MORE EXPRESSIONS

- ## 좋아요.   *Good.*   ▸ *These are commonly used with "네.": "네, 좋아요.", "네, 맞아요.", "네, 그래요."*

- ## 맞아요.   *Right.*

- ## 그래요.   *Okay.*   ▸ *It means 'That's right.', 'Understood.' or 'I will do so.', all of which are ways to say yes.*

## EXPRESSIVE TIPS

*The most basic use of the word '네' is to answer to a call or say yes.*
   *e.g.,* "**밥 먹었어요***(Did you eat)?*" "**네.**"
*It is also used to agree to a request or command.*
   *e.g.,* "**담배 피우지 마세요***(Please don't smoke)."* "**네.**"
*Additionally, '네' can be used to lightly ask someone to repeat what they said.*
   *e.g.,* "**네? 뭐라고 하셨어요***(What did you say)?*"

# 아니요.

## No.

- *This is a word used to answer a question negatively, in a polite style.*
- *'아뇨' is also often used in its shortened form.*

## STRUCTURE

### 아니 + 요.

[Exclamation]
*No.*

*Indicates respect to the listener.*

▸ 아니요

## MORE EXPRESSIONS

– **안 돼요.** *No. I/you can't.*

– **싫어요.** *I don't like it.*
▸ *'싫다' means 'to not be fond of'. Using this word to refuse something gives quite a strong impression.*

– **괜찮아요.** *It's okay.*
▸ *When refusing something, '아니요, 괜찮아요.' is commonly used, similar in meaning to 'No, thank you.'*

## EXPRESSIVE TIPS

*The way of answering negative questions differs between English and Korean.*
*For example, to the question "김치 안 먹어요(Don't you eat kimchi)?", the answer could be*
*"네, 안 먹어요.(Yes, I don't eat it.)" or "아니요, 먹어요.(No, I eat it.)"*
*It's about answering whether the response to the question is yes or no.*

## 6. RESPONSES

# 그냥 그래요.

**So-so.**

- *It's used when the response is neither clearly yes nor no, just indicating that it is so.*
- *It can be used not only to questions about how someone is doing, but also to answer if food tastes good, or if a movie was enjoyable.*

## STRUCTURE

**그냥** ∨ **그래** + **요.**

[Adverb]
Just.

A shortened form of
'그리하여(in that way)'.

Indicates respect
to the listener.

▸ 그냥 그래요

## MORE EXPRESSIONS

– **저도 잘 몰라요.**    *I don't know well either.*

– **글쎄요.**    *Well.*    ▸ *It's used to express a vague or unclear attitude towards someone's question or request.*

– **별로예요.**    *Not really.*

## DIALOG GLIMPSES

**잘 지내요?**
*How are you?*

**글쎄요, 그냥 그래요.**
*Well, so-so.*

## 6. RESPONSES

# 잠깐만요.

**Wait a second.**

LISTEN & REPEAT

– This sentence literally means 'Only for a short time.'
– It is used when asking someone to wait for a moment, like when you're looking for your card in your wallet to make a payment or when you need to pause for a moment while walking with someone.

## STRUCTURE

| 잠깐 | + | 만 | + | 요. |
|---|---|---|---|---|

**[Noun]**
For a very short period of time.

**[Particle]**
Indicates specifying something exclusively.

Indicates respect to the listener.

▸ 잠깐만요

## MORE EXPRESSIONS

– 잠시만요.              *Just a moment.*        ▸ '잠시' *means 'a short time'.*

– 10분만요.             *Just ten more minutes.*

– 잠깐만 기다려 주세요.   *Please wait a moment.*   ▸ *In formal situations or when you want to be more polite, instead of saying '잠깐만요', it's better to use a full sentence.*

## EXPRESSIVE TIPS

*The verb '기다리다' means 'to wait'. Let's try using it with the other sentence structures we've learned before.*

**잠깐만 기다려 주시겠어요?**        *(Would you wait for a second, please?)*
**잠깐만 기다려 주실 수 있으세요?**   *(Could you please wait for a second, please?)*
**좀만 기다려 주실 수 있으세요?**     *(Could you please wait for a bit, please?)*

## 6. RESPONSES

# 그러니까요.

**Tell me about it.**

LISTEN & REPEAT
☑ ☐ ☐ ☐

- *This expression is used to show agreement or understanding in response to someone else's remarks, literally meaning 'So it is.' It's often shortened to '그니까요.'*
- *The ending '-니까' indicates that the preceding statement gives a reason or basis.*

## STRUCTURE

### 그러(하다)  +  -니까  +  요.

**[Adjective]**
To be the same as that.

**[Ending]**
Indicates reason or basis.

Indicates respect
to the listener.

▸ 그러니까요

## MORE EXPRESSIONS

- 제 말이요.   *That's what I am saying.*   ▸ *This sentence means '제 말이 그 말이에요 (That's exactly what I'm saying).' expressing strong agreement with what someone else has said.*

- 그럴 수 있어요.   *It happens.*

- 무슨 말인지 알겠어요.   *I understand what you're saying.*

## DIALOG GLIMPSES

**그분은 왜 안 와요?**
*Why isn't he/she coming?*

**그러니까요!**
*Tell me about it!*

# 여기요.

Here.

- *You can say this, like 'Here it is.', when handing something to someone.*
- *In places like restaurants, it can also mean 'Please look here.' when placing an order.*

## STRUCTURE

여기     +     요.

[Pronoun]
Here.

*Indicates respect
to the listener.*

▸ 여기요

## MORE EXPRESSIONS

- 이거 받으세요.     *Please take this.*

- 여기 있어요.     *It's here.*

- 못 찾겠어요.     *I can't find it.*

## DIALOG GLIMPSES

여권 주세요.
*Give me your passport, please.*

여기요.
*Here it is.*

# 진짜요?

**Really?**

LISTEN & REPEAT

- *'진짜'* refers to something that is real, not fake.
- *You can use this expression to respond while listening to someone else.*

## STRUCTURE

**진짜** + **요?**

*[Noun]*
*Real.*

*Indicates respect to the listener.*

▸ 진짜요

## MORE EXPRESSIONS

- **정말요?**    *Seriously?*    ▸ *'정말' means 'words that are true and not false'.*

- **그래요?**    *Is it?*

- **뭐라고요?**    *What did you say?*    ▸ *It can be also used to ask again when you didn't hear what someone said, but asking this way is a bit blunt. To ask politely, you can say, '뭐라고 하셨어요?'*

## EXPRESSIVE TIPS

*The sentences on this page are not really questions that need an answer but are more about agreeing or acknowledging, so you don't actually need to respond to the question.*
*Instead of questioning the truth, it's often used to show you are actively listening or to express surprise in response to someone else's statement.*

# In Korean, how does a dog bark and how do stars shine?

 **멍멍** *The sound of a dog barking.*

e.g., **개가 멍멍 짖어요.**
*(The dog barks 'woof woof'.)*

 **야옹** *The sound of a cat meowing.*

e.g., **고양이가 야옹 울어요.**
*(The cat meows 'meow'.)*

 **꼬끼오** *The sound of a rooster crowing.*

e.g., **닭이 꼬끼오 울어요.**
*(The rooster crows 'cock-a-doodle-doo'.)*

 **똑똑** *The sound of tapping a hard object lightly and repeatedly.*

e.g., **문을 똑똑 두드려요.**
*(Knocking on the door 'knock knock'.)*

 **꼬르륵** *The sound of the stomach growling because of hunger or indigestion.*

e.g., **배고파서 꼬르륵거려요.**
*(The stomach growls 'gurgle' from hunger.)*

 **훌쩍훌쩍** *The sound or action of constantly sniffing.*

e.g., **동생이 훌쩍훌쩍 울어요.**
*(The younger sibling cries 'sniff sniff'.)*

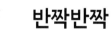 **반짝반짝** *The appearance of small lights flickering on and off in quickly.*

e.g., **별이 반짝반짝 빛나요.**
*(The stars twinkle 'twinkle twinkle'.)*

 **살랑살랑** *The appearance of the wind blowing lightly and repeatedly.*

e.g., **봄바람이 살랑살랑 불어요.**
*(The spring breeze blows 'gently gently'.)*

 **빙글빙글** *The action of turning in large circles repeatedly.*

e.g., **팽이가 빙글빙글 돌아요.**
*(The top spins 'round and round'.)*

# 저 친구 만났어요.

**I met a friend.**

LISTEN & REPEAT

- The ending '-았/었/했-' indicates the past tense.
- The past tense ending '-았/었/했-' goes between the stem and the sentence-closing ending, and is shortened according to the form of the preceding word.

## STRUCTURE

**저** ∨ **친구** ∨ **만나**(다) + **-았-** + **-어요.**

[Pronoun]
The humble form
of '나(I)'.

[Noun]
Friend.

[Verb]
To meet.

[Ending]
Expresses
the past tense.

[Ending]
Expresses
informal polite style.

▸ 저(는) 친구(를) 만**나았**어요 → 저 친구 만**났**어요

## MORE EXPRESSIONS

- 저 친구 **만들**었어요.  *I made a friend.*

- 저 친구 **불렀**어요.  *I called a friend.*
  - ▸ -었-: Added to letters whose vowel is not ㅏ/ㅗ.
  - ▸ 부르(다) + -었- + -어요 → 부르ㄹ + -었어요 → 부르ㄹ었어요 → 불렀어요 *(Refer to rule number 4 on page 63.)*

- 저 친구 **필요했**어요.  *I needed a friend.*
  - ▸ -했-: Added to letters before 하다.
  - ▸ 필요(하다) + -했- + -어요 → 필요했어요

## DIALOG GLIMPSES

**어제 뭐 했어요?**
*What did you do yesterday?*

**저 친구 만났어요.**
*I met a friend.*

# 그 사람은 경찰이었어요.

**The person was a police officer.**

- *Attaching the past tense ending '-었-' after '이다', which follows a noun, indicates the past tense.*
- *'그 사람' means 'the person' and does not specify the gender. The honorific form of '그 사람' is '그분'.*
- *The prenouns '이/저/그' respectively mean 'this/that/the' and modify the content of a noun in front of the noun.*

## STRUCTURE

그 ∨ 사람 + 은 ∨ 경찰 + 이(다) + -었- + -어요.

| | | | | | | |
|---|---|---|---|---|---|---|
| [Prenoun] The. | [Noun] Person. | [Particle] Indicates the topic of the sentence. | [Noun] Policeman. | Attached after a noun to describe it. | [Ending] Expresses the past tense. | [Ending] Expresses informal polite style. |

▸ 그 사람은 경찰이었어요

## MORE EXPRESSIONS

- **이** 사람은 **선생님**이었어요.  *This person was a teacher.*

- **저** 사람은 **남자 친구**였어요.  *That person was my boyfriend.*

  ▸ *When the letter preceding '이었어요' ends in a vowel, '이었어요' is shortened to '였어요'.*

- **저** 사람은 **여자 친구**였어요.  *That person was my girlfriend.*

## EXPRESSIVE TIPS

*Usually, '남자 친구' and '여자 친구' refer to someone you are romantically involved with. To distinguish between someone who is just a friend, people now wittily include '사람'(meaning 'person'), saying '남자 사람 친구' and '여자 사람 친구', which are commonly shortened to '남사친' and '여사친'. You can say it like this:*

A: **누구예요? 남자 친구예요?**  *(Who's that? Your boyfriend?)*
B: **아니요, 그냥 남사친이에요.**  *(No, just a male friend.)*

# 지금 티브이 보고 있어요.

**I'm watching TV now.**

LISTEN & REPEAT
✓ ☐ ☐ ☐

- *The pattern '-고 있다' indicates that an action is currently in progress.*
- *The pattern '-고 있다' can also be used to indicate the current state of wearing something, like clothes or shoes, not just for ongoing actions.*

## STRUCTURE

**지금** ∨ **티브이** ∨ **보**(다) + **-고 있**(다) + **-어요.**

[Adverb]
Now.

[Noun]
TV. Television.

[Verb]
To watch.

[Pattern]
Expresses that an action is currently in progress.

[Ending]
Expresses informal polite style.

▸ 지금 티브이(를) 보고 있어요 → 지금 티브이 보고 있어요

## MORE EXPRESSIONS

- 지금 **쉬**고 있어요.  *I'm taking a break now.*

- 지금 **밥 먹**고 있어요.  *I'm having a meal now.*

- 지금 **책 읽**고 있어요.  *I'm reading a book now.*

▸ *It is commonly used to indicate the present continuous tense even without the word '지금'.*

## EXPRESSION SKETCHES

티브이 봐요.

쉬어요.

밥 먹어요.

책 읽어요.

# 이건 내일 할 거예요.

**I will do this tomorrow.**

LISTEN & REPEAT
✓ ☐ ☐ ☐

– The pattern '-ㄹ/을 거예요' expresses guesses, plans, or intentions about the future.
– '이건/저건/그건' are respectively the shortened forms of '이거는/저거는/그거는', meaning 'this/that/the thing is'. '이거는/저거는/그거는' are spoken forms of '이것은/저것은/그것은'.

## STRUCTURE

**이건** ∨ **내일** ∨ **하**(다) + **-ㄹ 거**(다) + **이**(다) + **-에요.**

A shortened form of '이거는(this is)'.

[Adverb]
Tomorrow.

[Verb]
To do.

[Pattern]
Expresses plans, intentions about the future.

Attached after a noun to describe it.

[Ending]
Expresses informal polite style.

▸ 이건 내일 **하ㄹ** 거**이**에요 → 이건 내일 **할** 거**예**요

## MORE EXPRESSIONS

– **이 옷**은 내일 **입**을 거예요.

*I will wear these clothes tomorrow.*
▸ -을 거다: *Added to letters ending in a consonant.*
▸ 입(다) + -을 거예요 → 입을 거예요

– **이 신발**은 내일 **신**을 거예요.

*I will wear these shoes tomorrow.*

– **이 맛집**은 내일 **찾아갈** 거예요.

*I will visit this famous restaurant tomorrow.*
▸ 맛*(taste)* + 집*(house)*

## EXPRESSIVE TIPS

*When talking about future plans or intentions, the speaker's thoughts or will are naturally included. From this perspective, this expression is also used when making guesses or predictions based on personal experience or assumptions. For example,*

**'이 집 떡볶이는 맛있을 거예요**(This restaurant's tteokbokki will be delicious).'
**'그 사람 여자 친구는 예쁠 거예요**(His girlfriend will be pretty).'

# The conjugation of this word seems different from others!

*When verbs or adjectives are conjugated, special rules apply based on* the final letter of the stem and *the first letter of the ending* they are combined with. The first two rules are consistent across all forms, but other rules may only apply to specific verbs or adjectives, with some exceptions. Instead of memorizing these rules in advance, it's better to get familiar with them as you encounter verbs or adjectives with unusual conjugations during your learning process. Here are some of the most common rules:

1. '—' + '-아/어' → ○ + '-아/어'　　　　　※ *No exceptions.*

   *e.g.,* 크다*(to be big)* + -어요 → ㅋ어요 → 커요

   　　바쁘다*(to be busy)* + -았어요 → 바쁘았어요 → 바빴어요

2. 'ㄹ' + '-ㄴ/ㅂ/ㅅ/오' → ○ + '-ㄴ/ㅂ/ㅅ/오'　　※ *No exceptions.*

   *e.g.,* 살다*(to live)* + -는 것 같아요 → 사는 것 같아요

   　　만들다*(to make)* + -시- + -어요 → 만드시어요 → 만드세요

3. 'ㅅ' + *Vowels* → ○ + *Vowels*

   *e.g.,* 낫다*(to be better)* + -아요 → 나아요

   　　붓다*(to swell)* + -었어요 → 부었어요

4. '르' + '-아/어' → 'ㄹㄹ' + '-아/어'

   *e.g.,* 다르다*(to be different)* + -아요 → 다ㄹㄹ아요 → 달라요

   　　모르다*(to not know)* + -았어요 → 모ㄹㄹ았어요 → 몰랐어요

5. 'ㄷ' + *Vowels* → 'ㄹ' + *Vowels*

   *e.g.,* 듣다*(to listen)* + -어요 → 들어요

   　　걷다*(to walk)* + -었어요 → 걸었어요

6. 'ㅂ' + *Vowels* → '우' + *Vowels*　　　　※ *In cases* '돕다, 곱다', 'ㅂ' *changes to* '오', *not* '우'

   *e.g.,* 맵다*(to be spicy)* + -어요 → 매우어요 → 매워요

   　　춥다*(to be cold)* + -었어요 → 추우었어요 → 추웠어요

   　　돕다*(to help)* + -아요 → 도오아요 → 도와요

# 저는 한국어도 배워요.

**I also learn Korean.**

LISTEN & REPEAT
☑ ☐ ☐ ☐

– The particle '도' indicates addition or inclusion to something already present.
– It can be attached to any sentence element that needs its meaning, such as the subject, object, or adverb.

## STRUCTURE

저 + 는 ∨ 한국어 + 도 ∨ 배우(다) + -어요.

| [Pronoun] | [Particle] | [Noun] | [Particle] | [Verb] | [Ending] |
|---|---|---|---|---|---|
| The humble form of '나(I)'. | Indicates the topic of the sentence. | Korean language. | Indicates addition to something already present. | To learn. | Expresses informal polite style. |

▸ 저는 한국어도 배**우어**요 → 저는 한국어도 배**워**요

## MORE EXPRESSIONS

– 저**도** 한국어를 배워요.　　*I learn Korean, too.*

– 남편은 한국어**도** 배워요.　　*My husband also learns Korean.*

– 남편**도** 한국어를 배워요.　　*My husband learns Korean, too.*

## EXPRESSIVE TIPS

*Particles are attached directly after the word they affect, so when auxiliary particles, which add special meaning to the preceding word, are used, it is exactly the word before the particle that takes on the meaning.*
*When '도' is used instead of the topic or subject/object particles, it is used by itself. However, for other particles, '도' is added after them without omission. For example, '도' is used after the original particle, as in* **'저는 저녁에도 운동해요***(I also exercise in the evening)'* **or '저는 집에서도 공부해요***(I also study at home)'.*

# 저는 영어만 가르쳐요.

I teach only English.

LISTEN & REPEAT

- The particle '만' indicates specifying something exclusively.
- '만' can also be used with other particles, but one difference from the particle '도' is that '만' can be placed before '은/는', '이/가', '을/를' without being omitted. For example, 'N만은/만이/만을/에만/에서만'.

## STRUCTURE

**저** + **는** ∨ **영어** + **만** ∨ **가르치**(다) + **-어요.**

[Pronoun]
The humble form of '나(I)'.

[Particle]
Indicates the topic of the sentence.

[Noun]
English.

[Particle]
Indicates specifying something exclusively.

[Verb]
To teach.

[Ending]
Expresses informal polite style.

▸ 저는 영어만 가르**치어**요 → 저는 영어만 가르**쳐**요

## MORE EXPRESSIONS

- **저만** 영어를 가르쳐요.

  Only I teach English.

  ▸ It means 'I'm the only one who teaches English.'

- **아내만** 영어를 가르쳐요.

  Only my wife teaches English.

- 아내도 영어**만** 가르쳐요.

  My wife teaches only English, too.

  ▸ '아내만 영어도 가르쳐요.' means 'Only my wife also teaches English.'

## DIALOG GLIMPSES

스페인어도 가르치세요?
*Do you also teach Spanish?*

아뇨, 저는 영어만 가르쳐요.
*No, I teach only English.*

## 8. PARTICLES ② N하고 N(하고) 가져오세요. Please bring N and N.

# 연필하고 지우개하고 가져오세요.

**Please bring a pencil and an eraser.**

LISTEN & REPEAT
✓ ☐ ☐ ☐

### STRUCTURE ······················································

# 연필 + 하고 ∨ 지우개 + 하고 ∨ 가져오(다) + -시- + -어요.

| [Noun]<br>Pencil. | [Particle]<br>Connects two or more nouns of equal status. | [Noun]<br>Eraser. | [Particle]<br>Connects two or more nouns of equal status. | [Verb]<br>To bring. | [Ending]<br>Expresses honorific. | [Ending]<br>Expresses informal polite style. |

▶ 연필하고 지우개하고 가져오**시어**요 → 연필하고 지우개하고 가져오**세**요.

### MORE EXPRESSIONS ·············································

- **칫솔하고 치약(하고) 가져오세요.**     *Please bring a toothbrush and a toothpaste.*

- **과자하고 맥주(하고) 가져오세요.**     *Please bring snacks and beer.*

- **숟가락하고 젓가락(하고) 가져오세요.**     *Please bring a spoon and chopsticks.*

### EXPRESSION SKETCHES

**연필하고 지우개**     **칫솔하고 치약**     **과자하고 맥주**     **숟가락하고 젓가락**

## 8. PARTICLES ②   저한테 V-세요. Please V me.

# 저한테 물어보세요.

**Please ask me.**

LISTEN & REPEAT
☑ ☐ ☐ ☐

- *The particle '한테' indicates who an action is for or directed towards, commonly used in spoken language.*
- *Using just the predicate makes it a command. However, adding the honorific ending '-시/으시-' turns it into a more polite request or piece of advice.*

### STRUCTURE

**저** + **한테** ∨ **물어보**(다) + **-시-** + **-어요.**

[Pronoun]
The humble
form of '나(I)'.

[Particle]
Indicates who an action
is for or directed towards.

[Verb]
To ask.

[Ending]
Expresses honorific.

[Ending]
Expresses
informal polite style.

▸ 저한테 물어보**시어**요 → 저한테 물어보**세**요

### MORE EXPRESSIONS

- **저한테 전화하세요.**   *Please call me.*

- **저한테 맡기세요.**   *Please leave it to me.*

- **저한테 던지세요.**   *Please throw it to me.*

### EXPRESSIVE TIPS

*The particle '한테' is used to indicate that an action affects a certain target, meaning it is used with verbs that imply some movement from A to B. For example, verbs like '가다(to go)', '오다(to come)', '주다(to give)', '받다(to receive)', '말하다(to speak)', '듣다(to listen)', '가르치다(to teach)', '설명하다(to explain)', and '보내다(to send)' suggest something moving towards a target.*
*'한테' is very casual, and '에게' is used in written language. If the word before '한테' refers to someone higher in status, use '께'. For example, 선생님께 가세요(Please go to your teacher).*

# 저는 친구랑 놀았어요.
**I hung out with my friend.**

LISTEN & REPEAT

– The particle '랑/이랑' indicates a companion involved in an action.
– It is also used to indicate comparison or a standard for comparison. For example, '저는 아빠랑 닮았어요(I look just like my dad).'

## STRUCTURE

저 + 는 ∨ 친구 + 랑 ∨ 놀(다) + -았- + -어요.

| [Pronoun] | [Particle] | [Noun] | [Particle] | [Verb] | [Ending] | [Ending] |
|---|---|---|---|---|---|---|
| The humble form of '나(I)'. | Indicates the topic of the sentence. | Friend. | Indicates a companion involved in an action. | To play/hang out. | Expresses the past tense. | Expresses informal polite style. |

▸ 저는 친구랑 놀았어요

## MORE EXPRESSIONS

– 저는 친구랑 **싸웠**어요.　　*I had a fight with my friend.*

– 저는 친구들이랑 **약속했**어요.　*I made a promise with my friends.*

– 저는 친구들이랑 **헤어졌**어요.　*I said goodbye to my friends.*

▸ 들 indicates plural. And added after nouns regardless of the preceding word's form.
▸ 이랑: Added to letters ending in a consonant.

## EXPRESSIVE TIPS

*The particle '랑/이랑', like '하고', connects two or more nouns of equal status as conjunction particles. '하고' is also used to indicate a companion or object involved in the same action, just like '랑/이랑'. You can say that "연필이랑 지우개(랑) 가져오세요." or "저는 친구하고 놀았어요." Both are commonly used in spoken language, and there isn't a significant difference in meaning, but '랑/이랑' feels a bit more casual. For reference, '와/과' which has the same function, is mainly used in written language.*

# 집으로 가는 길이에요.

**I'm on my way home.**

LISTEN & REPEAT

---

- *The particle '로/으로' indicates the direction of movement.*
- *The modifier forming ending '-는/ㄴ/은' allows verbs or adjectives to modify nouns in the present tense.*
  *For example, '가(다) + -는 → 가는' can modify the following noun.*

## STRUCTURE

**집** + **으로** ∨ **가(다)** + **-는** ∨ **길** + **이(다)** + **-에요.**

| [Noun] | [Particle] | [Verb] | [Ending] | [Noun] | | [Ending] |
|---|---|---|---|---|---|---|
| House, Home. | Indicates the direction of movement. | To go. | Allows predicates to modify nouns in the present tense. | Way. | Attached after a noun to describe it. | Expresses informal polite style. |

▸ 집으로 가는 길이에요

## MORE EXPRESSIONS

- **학교로 가는 길이에요.**    *I'm on my way to school.*    ▸ 로: *Added to letters ending in a vowel or ㄹ.*

- **공항으로 가는 길이에요.**    *I'm on my way to the airport.*

- **술집으로 가는 길이에요.**    *I'm on my way to the bar.*    ▸ 술(alcohol) + 집(house)

## EXPRESSION SKETCHES

**집**

**학교**

**공항**

**술집**

# How do Koreans call the person in front of them?

*Foreigners in Korea might find it confusing to address someone directly in front of them because there's no universal second-person pronoun like 'you' in English.*

*'너' can be used for friends or juniors, and '당신' is not a polite equivalent. Though '당신' is correct as a respectful term in written language, it is uncommon to use '당신' in everyday conversation.*
*So, if you're not close enough to call someone '너' or by their name, what should you call the person in front of you?*

*In Korea, when addressing someone, it's common to avoid calling them directly like '**여기요**(Here).', '**저기요**(There).', or simply omitting the subject like '점심 먹었어요(Ate lunch)?'*

*The most common approach is to use specific occupational or family titles, even if the person does not actually hold that occupation. While this might feel awkward to foreigners, it is a form of respect and consideration widely used.*
*It's not unusual to call a stranger passing by on the street '**선생님**(teacher).' or '**사장님**(boss).' If they look young, you might call them '**학생**(student).'*

*Family terms like '형, 오빠, 언니, 누나' are used among individuals, and it's common to use '**아버님**(father)' or '**어머님**(mother)' for strangers.*
*In places like restaurants, it is also common to add '님' to '**이모**(aunt)', calling them '**이모님**'.*
*You might call strangers '**할아버지**(grandfather)', '**할머니**(grandmother)', or, regardless of gender, refer to them respectfully as '**어르신**(elder).'*

*In the workplace, titles or job positions are primarily used, such as '**대리님**(Assistant Manager).', '**과장님**(Manager).', or if there is no specific title, '◯(first name or full name) **님** or **씨**.'*

## 9. NEGATION 그분은 N이/가 아니에요. He/she is not N.

# 그분은 한국인이 아니에요.

**He/she is not Korean.**

LISTEN & REPEAT

– Attach '**N이/가 아니다**' to the noun when forming a negative sentence from a statement that ends with '**이다**' after a noun. For example, '**나는 학생이다**(I'm a student).' → '**나는 학생이 아니다**(I'm not a student).'
– The particle '**이/가**' used with '**아니다**' indicates that the preceding word is the complement, not the subject.

## STRUCTURE ·········································································

# 그분 + 은 ∨ 한국인 + 이 ∨ 아니(다) + -에요.

**[Pronoun]**
The honorific of '그 사람(the person)'.

**[Particle]**
Indicates the topic of the sentence.

**[Noun]**
Korean (person).

**[Particle]**
Indicates the complement.

**[Adjective]**
To not be.

**[Ending]**
Expresses informal polite style.

▸ 그분은 한국인이 아니에요

## MORE EXPRESSIONS ·······························································

– 그분은 **직원**이 아니에요.  *He/she is not an employee.*

– 그분은 **바보**가 아니에요.  *He/she is not a fool.*

– 그분은 **부자**가 아니에요.  *He/she is not a rich person.*

## DIALOG GLIMPSES

그분은 한국인이에요?
*Is he/she Korean?*

아뇨, 그분은 한국인이 아니에요.
*No, he/she is not Korean.*

# 저는 안 힘들어요.

**I'm not tired.**

- To negate a sentence with a verb or adjective, the adverb '안' is usually placed before it.
- The adjective '힘들다' means 'to require a lot of effort'. It also means 'to be difficult to do something'. It can refer to a physical or mental difficulty.

## STRUCTURE

**저** ＋ **는** ∨ **안** ∨ **힘들(다)** ＋ **-어요.**

| | | | | |
|---|---|---|---|---|
| *[Pronoun]* | *[Particle]* | *[Adverb]* | *[Adjective]* | *[Ending]* |
| The humble form of '나(I)'. | Indicates the topic of the sentence. | Not. | To be hard/tough. | Expresses informal polite style. |

▸ 저는 안 힘들어요

## MORE EXPRESSIONS

- 저는 안 **바빠**요.  　*I'm not busy.*

- 저희는 안 **깨끗해**요.  　*We are not clean.*  　▸ 저희: *The humble form of '우리(we)'.*

- 저희는 안 **친해**요.  　*We are not close.*  　▸ *Adjectives ending in 하다 use 안 before the adjective for negation. However, '하다 verbs', which are created by attaching 하다 to a noun, place 안 before 하다, not before the noun. (e.g., 운동하다 → 운동 안 하다, not 안 운동하다)*

## DIALOG GLIMPSES

**괜찮아요?**
*Are you okay?*

**네, 저는 안 힘들어요.**
*Yes, I'm not tired.*

## 9. NEGATION 저는 못 V/A-아/어/해요. I can't V/A.

# 저는 못 걸어요.

**I can't walk.**

LISTEN & REPEAT
☑ ☐ ☐ ☐

- *While '안' expresses simple negation or opposition, the adverb '못' indicates an inability to do something or to reach a certain level or state.*
- *For the explanation on how '걷다' is conjugated to '걸어요', refer to the fifth rule on page 63.*

**STRUCTURE** ·················································································

**저** + **는** ∨ **못** ∨ **걷**(다) + **-어요.**

[Pronoun]
The humble
form of '나(I)'.

[Particle]
Indicates the topic
of the sentence.

[Adverb]
Cannot.

[Verb]
To walk.

[Ending]
Expresses
informal polite style.

▸ 저는 못 **걷**어요 → 저는 못 **걸**어요

**MORE EXPRESSIONS** ·····························································································

- 저는 못 **움직여**요.  *I can't move.*

- 저는 못 **찾았어**요.  *I couldn't find it.*

- 저는 **노래** 못 **해**요.  *I can't sing.*

▸ *The use of '못' is the same as the use of '안' for negating '하다 verbs'.*
▸ *When you say '못하다' without spaces, it can mean not only that you really can't do something due to circumstances, but it may also mean 'to not do well'.*

**EXPRESSIVE TIPS**

*The adverb '안' is used before verbs or adjectives to indicate negation or opposition, while '못' is used before verbs to show the inability to do something. Here's an example to make it clearer: If someone says '술(alcohol)을 안 마셔요.', it means they choose not to drink alcohol based on personal will. But if they say '술을 못 마셔요.', it means they can't drink alcohol due to external factors. This could be because they are taking medication, need to drive, or can't handle alcohol.*

# 늘지 마세요.

**Don't be late.**

LISTEN & REPEAT

- *The pattern '-지 말다' attached after a verb to express a prohibition of an action.*
- *Since it prohibits an action, it is not used with adjectives or '이다(to be)'. The word here '늘다' is an adjective, but it is also a verb meaning 'to be later than the appointed time'.*

## STRUCTURE

**늘**(다)   +   **-지 말**(다)   +   **-시-**   +   **-어요.**

[Verb]
To be later than
the appointed time.

[Pattern]
Expresses a prohibition.

[Ending]
Expresses honorific.

[Ending]
Expresses
informal polite style.

▸ 늘지 **말시어**요 → 늘지 **마시어**요 → 늘지 **마세**요

## MORE EXPRESSIONS

- **뛰**지 마세요.   *Don't run.*

- **바꾸**지 마세요.   *Don't change it.*

- **남기**지 마세요.   *Don't leave it.*

## EXPRESSION SKETCHES

늘지 마세요.       뛰지 마세요.       바꾸지 마세요.       남기지 마세요.

**KOREAN NATIVE VIBE TIPS**
*About Age in Korea*

# How do Koreans ask and answer about age?

*In Korea, knowing each other's age is more important than in other countries. It's not just about curiosity but because age determines how people address each other(언니, 오빠, 형, 누나 etc.) and influences their speaking style(Informal casual style, etc.). So, it's common to ask about age when you first meet, which can surprise many foreigners.*

*However, times are changing. People are more cautious about asking age and don't necessarily speak casually just because the other person is younger. Yet, asking and answering about age is still natural. Here are the most common sentences Koreans use to ask and answer about age.*

① **몇 살이세요?**  *Literally it means 'How many years old are you?'*

② **나이가 어떻게 되세요?**  *Literally it means 'How is it with age?'*

③ **몇 년생이세요?**  *Literally it means 'What birth year are you?' (년: 'year', 생: 'birth')*

④ **몇 학번이세요?**  *Literally it means 'What school number are you?' (학번: 'the year of university entry')*

*① is the most direct way to ask about age. '살' is a unit noun for counting age. ① can be used with peers, but it might feel rude with someone older. ② is also direct but feels more polite than ①. ② can be used with older people. ③ and ④ are more indirect ways of asking. ④ is mainly used in educational settings. Adding '혹시(By any chance)' or '실례지만(Excuse me, but)' at the beginning makes them more polite.*

*Answer to ①②*  **스물한 살이에요. / 스물하나요.**  *(I'm) 21 years old. / I'm 21.*

*Answer to ③*  **93(구삼)년생이에요. / 93(구삼)이요.**  *I was born in (19)93. / It's (19)93.*

*Answer to ④*  **09(공구)학번이에요. / 09(공구)요.**  *I'm in class (20)09. / It's (20)09.*

*For ① and ②, you can directly say your age. You can include '살' or just the number. In this case, you use native Korean numbers. For birth year or school number, use Sino-Korean numbers. Generally, you only say the last two digits of the year, and '93' is commonly read as '구삼(nine three)' rather than '구십삼(ninety-three)'.*

**10. EXPRESSIONS** V-ㄹ/을게요. I will V.

# 기다릴게요.
**I will wait.**

LISTEN & REPEAT

- The ending '-ㄹ/을게' expresses the speaker's promise or will to do an action.
- This expression is like making a promise to the listener, so it is mainly used in personal and casual situations rather than in formal settings. It is also used to show the speaker's willingness to do something.

## STRUCTURE

기다리(다)  +  -ㄹ게  +  요.

[Verb]
To wait.

[Ending]
Expresses the speaker's
promise or will.

Indicates respect
to the listener.

▸ 기다리**ㄹ**게요 → 기다릴게요

## MORE EXPRESSIONS

- **주문할**게요.  *I will order.*  ▸ You can say this to a staff member in a restaurant or cafe.

- **계산할**게요.  *I will pay.*  ▸ When you want to pay for someone else's meal, you can say, '제가 계산할게요.'

- **다녀올**게요.  *I will be right back.*  ▸ You can say this to the person who stays at home when you leave the house.

## DIALOG GLIMPSES

**화장실 좀 다녀올게요.**
*I'll go to the restroom for a bit.*

**네, 기다릴게요.**
*Ok, I will wait.*

# 한번 시도해 보세요.

**Just give it a try.**

LISTEN & REPEAT

- *The verb '보다' means 'to see', but when used in the pattern '-아/어/해 보다', it means to try something. It can also mean having experienced something before.*
- *The verb '시도하다' itself means 'to try', but saying '한번 해 봐요.' with this pattern has a similar meaning.*

## STRUCTURE

**한번** ∨ **시도**(하다) + **-해 보**(다) + **-시-** + **-어요.**

[Adverb]
*Just/once.*

[Verb]
*To try.*

[Pattern]
*Expresses trying something out.*

[Ending]
*Expresses honorific.*

[Ending]
*Expresses informal polite style.*

▸ 한번 시도해 보**시어**요 → 한번 시도해 보**세**요

## MORE EXPRESSIONS

- 한번 **웃**어 보세요.   *Just try smiling.*
- 한번 **씹**어 보세요.   *Just try chewing.*
- 한번 **생각해** 보세요.   *Just think about it.*

▸ -어 보다: *Added to letters whose vowel is not ㅏ/ㅗ.*

## EXPRESSIVE TIPS

*When '한 번' is written with a space, it keeps the meanings of '한(one)' and '번(time)', truly signifying exactly 'one time'. However, when written as one word '한번', it doesn't just mean a count of attempts but indicates 'trying something as a test' or 'doing something when there is an opportunity'.*
*Examples include '**한번 먹어 볼게요**(I'll try eating it).' and '**우리 밥 한번 같이 먹어요**(Let's have a meal together sometime).'*

# 놀이공원 가 본 적 있으세요?

**Have you ever been to an amusement park?**

LISTEN & REPEAT

- The pattern '-ㄴ/은 적이 있다' expresses having had a certain experience in the past. And '-아/어/해 보다' means not only trying something but also having experienced that action before.
- Therefore, this sentence focuses on asking whether or not one has had such an experience.

## STRUCTURE

### 놀이공원 ∨ 가(다) + -아 보(다) + -ㄴ 적(이) 있(다) + -으시- + -어요?

| [Noun] Amusement park. | [Verb] To go. | [Pattern] Expresses trying something out. | [Pattern] Expresses having had certain experience in the past. | [Ending] Expresses honorific. | [Ending] Expresses informal polite style. |

▸ 놀이공원(에) 가아 보ㄴ 적(이) 있으시어요 → 놀이공원 가 본 적 있으세요

## MORE EXPRESSIONS

- **노래방** 가 본 적 있으세요?    *Have you ever been to a singing room?*

- **치과** 가 본 적 있으세요?    *Have you ever been to the dentist?*

- **해외여행** 가 본 적 없으세요?    *Have you never been on an overseas trip?*

  ▸ '-ㄴ/은 적이 없다' expresses having never had certain experience.

## DIALOG GLIMPSES

놀이공원 가 본 적 있으세요?
*Have you ever been to an amusement park?*

아니요, 가 본 적 없어요.
*No, I've never been there.*

# 저 한국말 할 수 있어요.

**I can speak Korean.**

LISTEN & REPEAT

- The pattern '-ㄹ/을 수 있다' expresses the ability to do something or the possibility of a state.
- Foreign learners sometimes translate 'I can speak Korean.' to '한국말을 말할 수 있다.', but that sounds unnatural, like '말을 말하다.'

## STRUCTURE

저 ∨ 한국말 ∨ 하(다) + -ㄹ 수 있(다) + -어요.

| | | | | |
|---|---|---|---|---|
| **[Pronoun]** | **[Noun]** | **[Verb]** | **[Pattern]** | **[Ending]** |
| The humble form of '나(I)'. | Korean language. | To do. | Expresses the ability to do something. | Expresses informal polite style. |

▸ 저(**는**) 한국말(**을**) 하**ㄹ** 수 있어요 → 저 한국말 **할** 수 있어요

## MORE EXPRESSIONS

- 저 **운전할** 수 있어요.   *I can drive.*

- 저 **된장찌개 끓일** 수 있어요.   *I can cook doenjang jjigae.*

- 저는 **하늘을 날** 수 없어요.   *I can't fly in the sky.*

▸ '된장' is a traditional Korean paste made from soybeans.
▸ '끓이다' means 'to boil'.

▸ '-ㄹ/을 수 없다' expresses that something is not possible.

## EXPRESSION SKETCHES

**한국말을 해요.**

**운전을 해요.**

**된장찌개를 끓여요.**

**하늘을 날아요.**

# 좀 싱거운 것 같아요.

**It seems a bit bland.**

LISTEN & REPEAT

– The pattern '-는/ㄴ/은 것 같다' is used to express speculation in the present tense.
– It is also used to indirectly convey the speaker's thoughts. Because it's not too direct, this expression is used very often for when expressing personal thoughts or opinions.

## STRUCTURE

좀 ∨ 싱겁(다) + -ㄴ 것 같(다) + -아요.

[Adverb]
A shortened form of '조금(a little)'.

[Adjective]
To be bland.

[Pattern]
Expresses speculation in the present tense.

[Ending]
Expresses informal polite style.

▸ 좀 싱겁ㄴ 것 같아요 → 좀 싱거우ㄴ 것 같아요 → 좀 싱거운 것 같아요

## MORE EXPRESSIONS

– 좀 **뜨거운** 것 같아요.　　*It seems a bit hot.*

▸ Even when there's a strong conviction that something is really hot, it's common to say it this way.

– 좀 **큰** 것 같아요.　　*It seems a bit big.*

– 좀 **작은** 것 같아요.　　*It seems a bit small.*

▸ -은 것 같다: *Added to adjective stems ending in a consonant.*
▸ 작(다) + -은 것 같아요 → 작은 것 같아요

## EXPRESSION SKETCHES

싱거워요.

뜨거워요.

커요.

작아요.

# 잘 모르겠어요.

**I think I don't know well.**

LISTEN & REPEAT
☑ ☐ ☐ ☐

- *The ending '-겠-' indicates future speculation, the subject's will, or is used to express a polite or indirect manner of speaking.*
- *Saying '잘 모르겠어요.' sounds much less blunt than '잘 몰라요.'*

## STRUCTURE

### 잘   ∨   모르(다)   +   -겠-   +   -어요.

**[Adverb]**
*Well/properly/fully.*

**[Verb]**
*To not know.*

**[Ending]**
*Expresses a polite, indirect manner of speaking.*

**[Ending]**
*Expresses informal polite style.*

▸ 잘 모르겠어요

## MORE EXPRESSIONS

– **잘 알겠어요.**   *I think I <u>understand</u> well.*   ▸ *'알다', the opposite of '모르다', means 'to know'.*

– **못 믿겠어요.**   *I think I can't <u>believe</u> it.*

– **못 참겠어요.**   *I think I can't <u>stand</u> it.*

## DIALOG GLIMPSES

**여기 뭐가 맛있어요?**
*What's delicious here?*

**잘 모르겠어요.**
*I think I don't know well.*

# 백화점에 옷 사러 가요.
**I'm going to the department store to buy clothes.**

LISTEN & REPEAT
☑ ☐ ☐ ☐

– The ending '-러/으러' expresses the purpose of going or coming actions.
– Since the subject is not mentioned, this sentence could mean I'm going or suggesting the other person to come with me, depending on the tone.

**STRUCTURE** ·····································································

**백화점** + **에** ∨ **옷** ∨ **사**(다) + **-러** ∨ **가**(다) + **-아요.**

| [Noun] Department store. | [Particle] Indicates location. | [Noun] Clothes. | [Verb] To buy. | [Ending] Expresses the purpose of going or coming actions. | [Verb] To go. | [Ending] Expresses informal polite style. |

▸ 백화점에 옷(을) 사러 **가아**요 → 백화점에 옷 사러 **가**요

**MORE EXPRESSIONS** ·····································································

– 백화점에 **구두** 사러 가요.   *I'm going to the department store to buy shoes.*

– **학교**에 **공부하**러 가요.   *I'm going to school to study.*

– **공원**에 **사진 찍**으러 가요.   *I'm going to the park to take pictures.*

  ▸ -으러: Added to letters ending in a consonant.
  ▸ 찍(다) + -으러 → 찍으러

**EXPRESSIVE TIPS**

*The ending '-러/으러' is used to express the purpose of an action involving going or coming, so the verbs that connect with '-러/으러' usually indicate movement. The most commonly used verbs with '-러/으러' include '가다(to go)', '오다(to come)', and '다니다(to attend/go regularly)'.*
*Additionally, verbs like '들어가다(to enter)', '들어오다(to come in)', '나가다(to go out)', '나오다(to come out)', '내려가다(to go down)', '내려오다(to come down)', '올라가다(to go up)', '올라오다(to come up)', and '돌아다니다(to move around)' are also used with '-러/으러'.*

# 내일 만나기로 했어요.
**We decided to meet tomorrow.**

LISTEN & REPEAT
☑ ☐ ☐ ☐

- The pattern '-기로 하다' expresses a decision or promise to do something. It can be a promise with someone else or a promise to oneself. In the latter case, it shows determination.
- Since '내일' is used as an adverb, the time particle '에' is not attached.

## STRUCTURE

**내일** ˅ **만나**(다) + **-기로** (하다) + **-했-** + **-어요.**

[Adverb]
Tomorrow.

[Verb]
To meet.

[Pattern]
Expresses a decision
or promise to act.

[Ending]
Expresses the
past tense.

[Ending]
Expresses
informal polite
style.

▸ 내일 만나기로 했어요

## MORE EXPRESSIONS

- 내일 <u>듣</u>기로 했어요.

  *I decided to <u>listen</u> tomorrow.*

- 내일 <u>씻</u>기로 했어요.

  *I decided to <u>wash</u> tomorrow.*

- <u>머리</u>는 내일 <u>감</u>기로 했어요.

  *I decided to <u>wash my hair</u> tomorrow.*

▸ The key sentence
shows an
appointment with
someone else, while
these three sentences
show one's own
determination.

▸ For the body, use the verb '씻다',
and for hair, use '감다'.

## DIALOG GLIMPSES

친구 언제 만나기로 했어요?
*When are you going to meet your friend?*

내일 만나기로 했어요.
*We decided to meet tomorrow.*

# 오늘은 찜닭이 먹고 싶어요.

**I want to eat jjimdak today.**

LISTEN & REPEAT

- *The pattern '-고 싶다' expresses a desire to do something.*
- *In this sentence, the particles '은' and '이' emphasize the preceding words as auxiliary particles.*
  *'은' suggests a stronger craving today than other days, and '이' emphasizes the jjimdak over using '을'.*

## STRUCTURE

**오늘** + **은** ∨ **찜닭** + **이** ∨ **먹**(다) + **-고 싶**(다) + **-어요.**

| [Adverb] | [Particle] | [Noun] | [Particle] | [Verb] | [Pattern] | [Ending] |
|---|---|---|---|---|---|---|
| Today. | Indicates emphasis. | Braised spicy chicken. | Indicates emphasis. | To eat. | Expresses a desire to do something. | Expresses informal polite style. |

▸ 오늘은 찜닭이 먹고 싶어요

## MORE EXPRESSIONS

– 오늘은 **머리**가 **자르**고 싶어요.　*I want to cut my hair today.*

– 오늘은 **영화**가 **보**고 싶어요.　*I want to watch a movie today.*

– 오늘은 **한잔하**고 싶어요.

*I want to have a drink today.*

▸ *'한잔하다' doesn't literally mean drinking one glass; it means the event of drinking.*

## EXPRESSIVE TIPS

*In the sentence '머리가 자르고 싶어요', '머리' means 'hair(머리카락)', not 'head(머리)'. To be precise, it should be '머리카락을 자르고 싶어요', but people usually just say '머리'. It's like saying 'I did my hair today.' as in '나 오늘 머리했어'. This shows how a word can have multiple meanings.*
*Another example is '밥'. When Koreans ask '밥 먹었어요?' as a greeting, it means 'Have you had a meal?' not 'Have you eaten rice?'. It's not correct to answer '아니요, 밥 말고 라면 먹었어요(No, I ate ramyeon, not rice).'*

# How do address someone by their Korean name?

In Korea, it's common to use job titles or, in close relationships, family titles like '형, 오빠, 언니, 누나' to address someone(Refer to page 16.). When the relationship is close, it's also common to add the first name in front, like '준호 오빠', '정아 언니'. However, if the other person is younger, they aren't called '동생'. Sometimes, one might playfully say like '하나 동생', but it's not usual. It's possible to refer to someone as '동생', but it's not used directly as a title. When someone is younger or of the same age, and the relationship is close enough to use informal casual language(반말), names are called directly.
In English-speaking contexts, it's common to call someone by their first name, like shouting "Mike!". But in Korean, a particle '아/야' is attached to the name, depending on the last letter.
**If the name ends in a consonant, '아' is added; if it ends in a vowel, '야' is added.**

*When calling '이하준'*:  **하준아**!
*When calling '임지수'*:  **지수야**!

In sentences, when names are used without titles, '-이' **is added, if the name ends in a consonant, and nothing is added if it ends in a vowel.** *Because '-이' is added to names ending in consonants, making it '하준이' instead of just '하준', the following particle is one that comes after words ending in vowels.*

**하준이가 먹었어. / 하준이는 뭐 해? / 하준이를 만나요.**
**지수가 먹었어. / 지수는 뭐 해? / 지수를 만나요.**

*Simply calling '하준!' or '지수!' or using phrases like '하준이 먹었어. / 하준은 뭐 해? / 하준을 만나요.' is functional but can be a common error among foreign learners. So, if you have friends close enough to use their names directly, it's best to address and refer to them in this manner.*

## 11. USING ADVERBS  진짜 V/A-아/어/해요. I'm/it's really V/A.

# 진짜 힘들어요.
**I'm really tired.**

LISTEN & REPEAT

- *'진짜' is an adverb commonly used for emphasis, meaning 'truly' or 'really'.*
- *The '진짜' in '진짜요?' on page 57 is the same word as here. However, the '진짜' on page 57 is used as a noun, while in '진짜 힘들어요' here, it is used as an adverb to modify the whole sentence.*

## STRUCTURE

### 진짜  ∨  힘들(다)  +  -어요.

[Adverb]
*Really.*

[Adjective]
*To be tired/hard.*

[Ending]
*Expresses informal polite style.*

▸ 진짜 힘들어요

## MORE EXPRESSIONS

- **진짜 맛없어요.**  *It's really <u>not tasty</u>.*

- **진짜 대단해요.**  *It's really <u>amazing</u>.*  ▸ *'대단하다' means 'to be very severe/excellent.'*

- **진짜 완벽해요.**  *It's really <u>perfect</u>.*

## DIALOG GLIMPSES

**안 힘들어요?**
*Aren't you tired?*

**아니요, 진짜 힘들어요.**
*No, I'm really tired.*

## 11. USING ADVERBS  완전(히) V/A-아/어/해요.  It's so V/A.

# 완전(히) 멋있어요.

**It's so cool.**

LISTEN & REPEAT
✓ ☐ ☐ ☐

- *'완전히', the adverb form of '완전하다(to be complete)', means 'completely' or 'perfectly'.*
- *But in spoken language, '완전' is used as an adverb without '히', and it means 'much more than usual'.*

## STRUCTURE ··············································································

**완전**  ∨  **멋있**(다)  +  **-어요.**

[Adverb]
*Much more than usual.*

[Adjective]
*To be pleasing to look at/
to be excellent.*

[Ending]
*Expresses
informal polite style.*

▸ 완전**히** 멋있어요  →  완전 멋있어요

## MORE EXPRESSIONS ·······································································

- **완전 편**해요.    *It's so <u>comfortable</u>.*

- **완전 사랑스러워**요.    *She's so <u>lovely</u>.*    ▸ *'사랑하다' means 'to love',
and '-스럽다' adds 'having such a quality'
to a root, making it an adjective.*

- **완전 잘생겼**어요.    *He's so <u>handsome</u>.*

## EXPRESSIVE TIPS

*Even though '완전히' is the correct form, '완전' is often used as an adverb for emphasis. Using '완전' as an adverb is ungrammatical and is uncommon among older people or in formal situations. However, it is often used in everyday life.*
*'완전' is used with a meaning of 'very', but its original form '완전히' is used closer to its original meaning, such as '완전히 **끝났다**(It's completely finished).' or '완전히 **부서졌다**(It's totally destroyed).'*

# 너무 비싸요.

It's too expensive.

- '너무' is an adverb meaning 'beyond a certain degree or limit', but in conversation, it is often used for emphasis.
- So, for example, if you say '너무 비싸요', it means it's so expensive that you can't afford it.

## STRUCTURE

**너무**  V  **비싸(다)**  +  **-아요.**

[Adverb]
Too.

[Adjective]
To be expensive.

[Ending]
Expresses
informal polite style.

▸ 너무 비**싸아**요 → 너무 비**싸**요

## MORE EXPRESSIONS

- 너무 **더러워**요.  *It's too dirty.*  ▸ 더럽(다) + -어요 → 더러우어요 → 더러워요

- 너무 **더워**요.  *It's too hot.*  ▸ 덥(다) + -어요 → 더우어요 → 더워요

- 너무 **추워**요.  *It's too cold.*  ▸ 춥(다) + -어요 → 추우어요 → 추워요

## EXPRESSION SKETCHES

**비싸요.**

**더러워요.**

**더워요.**

**추워요.**

## 11. USING ADVERBS  빨리/천천히 V/A-아/어/해요.  V quickly/slowly.

# 빨리 타요.

**Get on quickly.**

LISTEN & REPEAT

- *'빨리' is an adverb meaning 'in a short amount of time.' or 'earlier than a certain standard or compared to another.'*
- *When boarding or riding transportation like cars, subways, airplanes, ships, or even horses, '타다' is used.*

## STRUCTURE

**빨리**  ∨  **타**(다)  +  **-아요.**

[Adverb]
*Quickly.*

[Verb]
*To ride/get on.*

[Ending]
*Expresses informal polite style.*

▸ 빨리 **타아**요 → 빨리 **타**요

## MORE EXPRESSIONS

- **빨리 자**요.    *Go to sleep quickly.*

- **천천히 와**요.    *Come slowly.*    ▸ *When you are waiting at the meeting place ahead of time, you can say this to mean 'Take your time.'*

- **천천히 걸**어요.    *Walk slowly.*    ▸ 걷(다) + -어요 → 걸 + -어요 → 걸어요

## DIALOG GLIMPSES

**저기 택시가 기다리고 있어요.**
*There's a taxi waiting over there.*

**빨리 타요.**
*Get on quickly.*

# 혹시 펜 있으세요?

**Do you have a pen by any chance?**

LISTEN & REPEAT
✓ ☐ ☐ ☐

- '혹시' means 'although it seems unlikely, just in case', and is used in questions to mean 'thought to be so, but not certain'. It is used when hesitating to ask about something you're unsure of.
- It's used to cautiously ask someone about something when the speaker is uncertain.

## STRUCTURE

| 혹시 | ∨ | 펜 | ∨ | 있(다) | + | -으시- | + | -어요? |
|------|---|-----|---|--------|---|--------|---|--------|

[Adverb]
By any chance/maybe.

[Noun]
Pen.

[Verb]
To have.

[Ending]
Expresses honorific.

[Ending]
Expresses informal polite style.

▸ 혹시 펜(**이**) 있으**시어**요 → 혹시 펜 있으**세**요

## MORE EXPRESSIONS

– 혹시 **종이** 있으세요?  *Do you have paper by any chance?*

– 혹시 **동전** 있으세요?  *Do you have coins by any chance?*

– 혹시 **현금** 없으세요?  *You don't have cash by any chance?*  ▸ *When you're asking someone if they don't have something, use '없다' instead of '있다'.*

## EXPRESSION SKETCHES

**펜**

**종이**

**동전**

**현금**

## 11. USING ADVERBS  갑자기 N이/가 V/A-아/어/해요. Suddenly N V/A.

# 갑자기 비가 와요.

**Suddenly it's raining.**

LISTEN & REPEAT
✓ ☐ ☐ ☐

- '갑자기' is an adverb meaning 'suddenly, without time to think in advance.'
- '비가 와요' translates literally to 'Rain is coming'. '비가 내려요' is also used, meaning 'Rain is falling.'

**STRUCTURE** · · · · · · · · · · · · · · · · · · · · · · · · · · · · · · · · · · · · · · · · · · · · · · · · · · · · · · · · · · · · · · · · · · · · ·

### 갑자기  ∨  비  +  가  ∨  오(다)  +  아요.

| | | | | |
|---|---|---|---|---|
| *[Adverb]*<br>*Suddenly.* | *[Noun]*<br>*Rain.* | *[Particle]*<br>*Indicates the subject of the sentence.* | *[Verb]*<br>*To come.* | *[Ending]*<br>*Expresses informal polite style.* |

▸ 갑자기 비가 **오아**요 → 갑자기 비가 **와**요

**MORE EXPRESSIONS** · · · · · · · · · · · · · · · · · · · · · · · · · · · · · · · · · · · · · · · · · · · · · · · · · · · · · · · · · · · · · · ·

- 갑자기 **눈**이 **와**요.　　　*Suddenly it's snowing.*

- 갑자기 **일**이 **생겼어**요.　　*Suddenly something came up.*

- 갑자기 **약속**이 **생겼어**요.　*Suddenly I have an appointment.*

▸ '일' means 'work/job', but it also broadly means 'a thing that needs to be taken care of' or 'a problem that is causing issues'.

▸ '생기다' means 'to be newly formed where there was none before' and 'for some event to occur'.

**EXPRESSIVE TIPS**

*Here are some additional ways to describe the weather:*

**눈이/비가 내려요.** *Snow/rain is falling.*　　**너무 더워요.** *It's too hot.*　　**바람이 불어요.** *It's windy.*
**함박눈이 내려요.** *It's snowing heavily.*　　**너무 추워요.** *It's too cold.*　　**하늘이 흐려요.** *The sky is cloudy.*
**소나기가 내려요.** *It's showering.*　　**조금 쌀쌀해요.** *It's a bit chilly.*　　**날씨가 맑아요.** *The weather is clear.*

# 그냥 해 봐요.

**Just try it.**

LISTEN & REPEAT

- '그냥' is an adverb meaning 'as it is, doing nothing' or 'without any payment, condition, or meaning.'
  "그냥요(Just because)." can itself be an answer.
- The pattern '-아/어/해 보다', it indicates trying something out.

## STRUCTURE

**그냥**  ∨  (하다)  +  **-해 보**(다)  +  **-아요.**

*[Adverb]*
Just.

*[Verb]*
To do.

*[Pattern]*
Expresses
trying something out.

*[Ending]*
Expresses
informal polite style.

▸ 그냥 해 **보아**요  →  그냥 해 **봐**요

## MORE EXPRESSIONS

- **다시** 해 봐요.      *Try again.*

- **혼자** 해 봐요.      *Try it by yourself.*      ▸ '혼자' is used both as a noun meaning 'alone' and
                                                      as an adverb meaning 'without the help of others.'

- **스스로** 해 봐요.    *Try it on your own.*      ▸ '스스로' is used both as a noun meaning 'oneself' and
                                                      as an adverb meaning 'on one's own.'

## DIALOG GLIMPSES

**제가 할 수 있을까요?**
*Do you think I can do it?*

**그냥 해 봐요.**
*Just try it.*

# Do Koreans attach 이/가 or 을/를 to adverbs as well?

*Previously, it was explained that '은/는' can mark the topic of a sentence and also convey a contrasting meaning. However, '이/가' and '을/를' can also act as auxiliary particles, adding special meaning.*
*Often, '이/가' or '을/를' can be omitted when they simply indicate the subject or object. However, when used explicitly, they might be playing a special role: to focus and emphasize the preceding word. For example:*

① **저 경찰이에요**. / ② **제가 경찰이에요**. *I am a police officer.*

*① is what you might say in response to "What's your job?". But in ②, '이/가' is used, spotlighting '저(I)' right before it, implying it is 'I', who is the police officer. If someone asks the person next to you, "Are you a police officer?" you might reply, "그분이 아니라 제가 경찰이에요.(It's not him; I am the police officer.)", or in response to "Is there a police officer here?" you might say, "제가 경찰이에요(I am the police officer)." Using "그분이 아니라 저는 경찰이에요." or "저는 경찰이에요." might sound awkward in these situations.*

① **커피 안 마셔요**? / ② **커피를 안 마셔요**? *You don't drink coffee?*

*① is a general question about whether the person drinks coffee. But ② adds '을/를', emphasizing '커피'. If '을/를' were just indicating '커피' as the object of '마시다', it would usually be omitted. This suggests there's context making '커피' worth emphasizing. If someone says "I don't drink coffee.", you might respond, "오, 정말요? 커피를 안 마셔요? 그 맛있는 걸?(Oh, really? You don't drink coffee? That delicious thing?)" or if someone who usually drinks five cups a day says, "I don't drink coffee anymore.", you might say "커피를 안 마셔요(You don't drink coffee)?"*

*When '이/가' or '을/를' act as auxiliary particles, they don't just attach to subjects or objects, nor do they always follow nouns. In sentences like "저는 김밥이 먹고 싶어요(I want to eat kimbap).", instead of using '을/를' after '김밥', the target of '먹고 싶다', '이/가' is used for emphasis. It doesn't make '김밥' the subject of the sentence. Similarly, '을/를' can follow adverbs, like in "저는 많이를 못 먹어요(I can't eat a lot).", emphasizing '많이'. saying, '저는 많이 못 먹어요.' is also correct, but adding '을/를' emphasizes '많이'.*

# GRAMMAR RECAP

*(In order of ㄱㄴㄷ)*

« PARTICLES »

## 도

*Indicates addition to something already present.*
*Added regardless of the preceding word's form.*

## 랑 / 이랑

*Indicates a companion involved in an action.*
랑: *Added to letters ending in a vowel.*
이랑: *Added to letters ending in a consonant.*

## 로 / 으로

*Indicates the direction of movement.*
로: *Added to letters ending in a vowel or ㄹ.*
으로: *Added to letters ending in a consonant.*

## 만

*Indicates specifying something exclusively.*
*Added regardless of the preceding word's form.*

## 에

*Indicates location and time.*
*Added regardless of the preceding word's form.*

## 에서

*Indicates a departure point or a place.*
*Added regardless of the preceding word's form.*

## 은 / 는

*Indicates the topic of the sentence or emphasis.*
은: *Added to letters ending in a consonant.*
는: *Added to letters ending in a vowel.*

## 을 / 를

*Indicates the object of the sentence or emphasis.*
을: *Added to letters ending in a consonant.*
를: *Added to letters ending in a vowel.*

## 이 / 가

*Indicates the subject of the sentence or emphasis.*
이: *Added to letters ending in a consonant.*
가: *Added to letters ending in a vowel.*

## 하고

*Connects two or more nouns of equal status.*
*Added regardless of the preceding word's form.*

## 한테

*Indicates who an action is for or directed towards.*
*Added regardless of the preceding word's form.*

« ENDINGS »

## -겠-

*Expresses subject's will or a polite, indirect manner of speaking.*
*Added to stems regardless of the preceding word's form.*

## -는 / -ㄴ / -은

*Allows verbs or adjectives to modify nouns in the present tense.*
-는: *Added to verb stems, and the stem of 있다/없다.*
-ㄴ: *Added to adjective stems ending in a vowel or ㄹ.*
-은: *Added to adjective stems ending in a consonant.*

## -ㄹ게 / -을게

*Expresses the speaker's promise or will to do an action.*
-ㄹ게: *Added to letters of the stem ending in a vowel or ㄹ.*
-을게: *Added to letters of the stem ending in a consonant.*

## -ㄹ까 / -을까

*Expresses asking for the listener's intent.*
-ㄹ까: *Added to letters of the stem ending in a vowel or ㄹ.*
-을까: *Added to letters of the stem ending in a consonant.*

## -러 / -으러

*Expresses the purpose of going or coming actions.*
-러: *Added to letters of the stem ending in a vowel or ㄹ.*
-으러: *Added to letters of the stem ending in a consonant.*

# -ㅂ니다 / -습니다

*Expresses formal polite style.*

-ㅂ니다: *Added to letters of the stem ending in a vowel or ㄹ.*
-습니다: *Added to letters of the stem ending in a consonant.*

# -시- / -으시-

*Expresses honorific.*

-시-: *Added to letters of the stem ending in a vowel or ㄹ.*
-으시-: *Added to letters of the stem ending in a consonant.*

# -아요 / -어요 / -해요 / -에요

*Expresses informal polite style.*

-아요: *Added to letters of the stem whose vowel is ㅏ/ㅗ.*
-어요: *Added to letters of the stem whose vowel is not ㅏ/ㅗ.*
-해요: *Added to letters before 하다.*
-에요: *Added to the stem of 이다/아니다.*

# -았- / -었- / -했-

*Expresses the past tense.*

-았-: *Added to letters of the stem whose vowel is ㅏ/ㅗ.*
-었-: *Added to letters of the stem whose vowel is not ㅏ/ㅗ.*
-했-: *Added to letters before 하다.*

« PATTERNS »

# -고 싶다

*Expresses a desire to do something.*
*Added to verb stems regardless of the preceding word's form.*

# -고 있다

*Expresses that an action is currently in progress.*
*Added to verb stems regardless of the preceding word's form.*

# -기로 하다

*Expresses a decision or promise to act.*
*Added to verb stems regardless of the preceding word's form.*

# -ㄴ / -은 적이 있다

*Expresses having had certain experience in the past.*

-ㄴ 적이 있다: *Added to letters of the stem ending in a vowel or ㄹ.*
-은 적이 있다: *Added to letters of the stem ending in a consonant.*

# -는 / -ㄴ / -은 것 같다

*Expresses speculation in the present tense.*

-는 것 같다: *Added to verb stems, and the stem of 있다/없다.*
-ㄴ 것 같다: *Added to adjective stems ending in a vowel or ㄹ.*
-은 것 같다: *Added to adjective stems ending in a consonant.*

# -ㄹ / -을 수 있다

*Expresses the ability to do something or the possibility of a state.*

-ㄹ 수 있다: *Added to letters of the stem ending in a vowel or ㄹ.*
-을 수 있다: *Added to letters of the stem ending in a consonant.*

# -ㄹ / -을 거다

*Expresses guesses, plans, or intentions about the future.*

-ㄹ 거다: *Added to letters of the stem ending in a vowel or ㄹ.*
-을 거다: *Added to letters of the stem ending in a consonant.*

# -아 / -어 / -해 보다

*Expresses trying something out.*

-아 보다: *Added to letters of the stem whose vowel is ㅏ/ㅗ.*
-어 보다: *Added to letters of the stem whose vowel is not ㅏ/ㅗ.*
-해 보다 : *Added to letters before 하다.*

# -아 / -어 / -해 주다

*Expresses doing an action for someone else.*

-아 주다: *Added to letters of the stem whose vowel is ㅏ/ㅗ.*
-어 주다: *Added to letters of the stem whose vowel is not ㅏ/ㅗ.*
-해 주다: *Added to letters before 하다.*

# -아도 / -어도 / -해도 되다

*Expresses permission or allowance for an action.*

-아도 되다: *Added to letters of the stem whose vowel is ㅏ/ㅗ.*
-어도 되다: *Added to letters of the stem whose vowel is not ㅏ/ㅗ.*
-해도 되다: *Added to letters before 하다.*

# -지 말다

*Expresses a prohibition of an action.*
*Added to verb stems regardless of the preceding word's form.*

# KEY TO KOREAN
한국어
# KOREAN
## DAILY BASIC
## CONVERSATION
### : 75 MUST-KNOW SENTENCE PATTERNS
# WORKBOOK

교육 R&D에 앞서가는
 키출판사

# KEY TO
# KOREAN
# DAILY BASIC
# CONVERSATION
## : 75 MUST-KNOW SENTENCE PATTERNS
# WORKBOOK

| Activities | Answers |
|---|---|
| 2~76 | 77~79 |

교육 R&D에 앞서가는

키출판사

# 안녕하세요?

❶ *Trace the sentences and practice your handwriting.*

안녕하세요?

안녕하세요?

❷ *Fill in the blank.*

**안녕하**(다) + - ⬚ - + -**어요?**

↑

*[Ending]*
*Expresses honorific.*

❸ *Write the sentences.*

*Hello?*

*Nice to meet you!*

반갑습니다!

❶ *Trace the sentences and practice your handwriting.*

감사합니다.

감사합니다.

❷ *Fill in the blanks.*

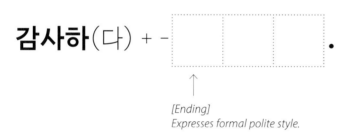

**감사하**(다) + - ⬜ ⬜ ⬜ .

↑

*[Ending]*
*Expresses formal polite style.*

❸ *Match the sentences.*

| | |
|---|---|
| *Thank you.* ● | ● a. 괜찮아요. |
| *It's not.* ● | ● b. 감사합니다. |
| *It's fine.* ● | ● c. 아니에요. |

# 죄송합니다.

❶ *Trace the sentences and practice your handwriting.*

죄송합니다.

죄송합니다.

❷ *Match the sentences.*

*Excuse me.* ●

*I'm sorry.* ●

*It's okay.* ●

● a. 죄송합니다.

● b. 실례합니다.

● c. 괜찮아요.

❸ *Write the sentences.*

*I'm sorry.*

*It's okay.*

괜찮아요.

❶ *Trace the sentences and practice your handwriting.*

잘 먹겠습니다.

잘 먹겠습니다.

❷ *Fill in the blank.*

# 잘 ˅ 먹(다) + - ⬚ - + -습니다.

↑

*[Ending]*
*Expresses subject's will.*

❸ *Look at the pictures and write in Korean as in the main book.*

*Enjoy your meal.*

*Thank you for the meal.*
*(after eating)*

*I'm full.*

*Thank you for the meal.*
*(before eating)*

# 안녕히 계세요.

❶ *Trace the sentences and practice your handwriting.*

안녕히 계세요.

안녕히 계세요.

❷ *Match the sentences.*

Goodbye. ⦿                    ⦿ a. 좋은 하루 보내세요.

Have a nice day. ⦿          ⦿ b. 안녕히 계세요.

See you later. ⦿             ⦿ c. 다음에 봐요.

❸ *Write the sentences.*

*Goodbye. (said by the person leaving).*

*You, too. Goodbye. (said by the person staying)*

네, 안녕히 가세요.

# 잘 지내셨어요?

**❶** *Trace the sentences and practice your handwriting.*

잘 지내셨어요?

잘 지내셨어요?

**❷** *Fill in the blanks.*

## 잘 ⌄ 지내(다) + -시- + -었- + - [ ] [ ] ?

↑

*[Ending]*
*Expresses informal polite style.*

**❸** *Match the sentences.*

| | |
|---|---|
| *Have you been well?*  ● | ●  a. 보고 싶었어요. |
| *Long time no see.*  ● | ●  b. 잘 지내셨어요? |
| *I missed you.*  ● | ●  c. 오랜만이에요. |

# 저는 마이클이에요.

❶ *Trace the sentences and practice your handwriting.*

저는 마이클이에요.

저는 마이클이에요.

❷ *Fill in the blanks.*

**저** + **는** ⌄ **마이클** + **이**(다) + ‒ [　] [　] **.**

↑

*[Ending]*
*Expresses informal polite style.*

❸ *Find a new word from a dictionary and make your own sentence.*

① *It is a noun.*
② *I'm this.*

**저는**  소피아  **이에요** / 예요 **.**

저는 소피아예요　　　　　 **.**

# 오빠는 잘 지내요?

❶ *Trace the sentences and practice your handwriting.*

오빠는 잘 지내요?

오빠는 잘 지내요?

❷ *Match the sentences.*

*Is your older brother doing well?* •

• a. **오빠는 잘 지내요?**

*Is your younger brother doing well?* •

• b. **부모님은 잘 지내세요?**

*Are your parents doing well?* •

• c. **동생은 잘 지내요?**

❸ *Look at the pictures and write the words in Korean.*

*older sister (used by females)*

*older brother (used by females)*

*older brother (used by males)*

*older sister (used by males)*

# 저는 김치를 먹어요.

2. PARTICLES ①
**MAIN BOOK page 17**

❶ *Trace the sentences and practice your handwriting.*

저는 김치를 먹어요.

저는 김치를 먹어요.

❷ *Fill in the blank.*

**저** + **는** ∨ **김치** + ☐ ∨ **먹**(**다**) + **-어요.**

↑

*[Particle]*
*Indicates the object*
*of the sentence.*

❸ *Find a new word from a dictionary and make your own sentence.*

① *It is a noun.*
② *I eat this.*

**저는** ☐ **을 / 를 먹어요.**

☐ .

❶ *Trace the sentences and practice your handwriting.*

여기는 커피가 맛있어요.

여기는 커피가 맛있어요.

❷ *Fill in the blank.*

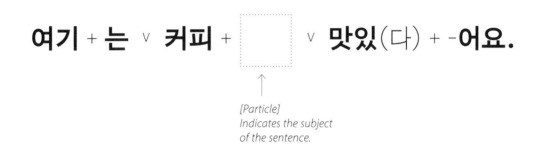

여기 + 는 ∨ 커피 + ☐ ∨ 맛있(다) + -어요.

↑
[Particle]
Indicates the subject
of the sentence.

❸ *Look at the pictures and write the words in Korean.*

| *gimbap* | *coffee* | *ramyeon* | *bulgogi* |
|---|---|---|---|

❶ *Trace the sentences and practice your handwriting.*

저는 서울에 살아요.

저는 서울에 살아요.

❷ *Fill in the blank.*

저 + 는 ∨ 서울 + [　　] ∨ 살(다) + -아요.

↑

*[Particle]*
*Indicates location.*

❸ *Find a new word from a dictionary and make your own sentence.*

① *It is a noun.*
② *I live here.*

저는 [　　　　　　] 에 살아요.

[　　　　　　　　　　　　　　　　　　] .

❶ *Trace the sentences and practice your handwriting.*

저는 아침에 운동해요.

저는 아침에 운동해요.

❷ *Look at the pictures and write the words in Korean.*

| night | morning | evening | noon |
|---|---|---|---|
| | | | |

❸ *Write the sentences.*

*Do you work out in the evening?*

저녁에 운동해요?

*No, I work out in the morning.*

아니요,

❶ *Trace the sentences and practice your handwriting.*

저는 미국에서 왔어요.

저는 미국에서 왔어요.

❷ *Fill in the blanks.*

**저** + **는** ∨ **미국** + [ ___ ___ ] ∨ **오**(다) + **-았-** + **-어요.**

↑

*[Particle]*
*Indicates a departure point*
*or a place.*

❸ *Find a new word from a dictionary and make your own sentence.*

① *It is a noun.*
② *I came from here.*

**저는** [ _____ ] **에서 왔어요.**

[ _____ ] **.**

❶ *Trace the sentences and practice your handwriting.*

가방 주세요.

가방 주세요.

❷ *Look at the pictures and write the words in Korean.*

| umbrella | bag | passport | mobile phone |
|---|---|---|---|

❸ *Find a new word from a dictionary and make your own sentence.*

① *It is a noun.*
② *I'm asking you to give me this.*

**주세요.**

.

❶ *Trace the sentences and practice your handwriting.*

이거 계산해 주세요.

이거 계산해 주세요.

❷ *Match the sentences.*

*Please exchange this.* •

*Please refund this.* •

*Please check this out.* •

a. 이거 환불해 주세요.

b. 이거 계산해 주세요.

c. 이거 교환해 주세요.

❸ *Write the sentences.*

*Please check this out.*

*Yes, please give it to me.*

❶ *Trace the sentences and practice your handwriting.*

안 맵게 해 주세요.

안 맵게 해 주세요.

❷ *Fill in the blank.*

☐ ∨ **맵게** + **해 주**(다) + **-시-** + **-어요.**

↑
*[Adverb]*
*Not.*

❸ *Match the sentences.*

*Please make it not sweet.* •                    • a. 안 짜게 해 주세요.

*Please make it not salty.* •                    • b. 안 맵게 해 주세요.

*Please make it not spicy.* •                    • c. 안 달게 해 주세요.

# 설탕 넣어 주시겠어요?

❶ Trace the sentences and practice your handwriting.

설탕 넣어 주시겠어요?

설탕 넣어 주시겠어요?

❷ Look at the pictures and write in Korean as in the main book.

| | | | |
|---|---|---|---|
| Add salt. | Take out the nuts. | Add sugar. | Take out the syrup. |
| | | | |

❸ Find a new word from a dictionary and make your own sentence.

① It is a noun.
② I'm asking you to add this.

넣어 주시겠어요?

?

❶ *Trace the sentences and practice your handwriting.*

반찬 좀 더 주실 수 있으세요?

반찬 좀 더 주실 수 있으세요?

❷ *Fill in the blank.*

⌐ ⌐
⌐ ⌐  ∨ **더** ∨ **주**(다) + **-시-** + **-ㄹ 수 있**(다) + **-으시-** + **-어요?**
⌐ ⌐
↑
[Adverb]
A little.

❸ *Match the sentences.*

Could you help me,
please?
•
• a. 길 좀 알려 주실 수 있으세요?

Could you tell me
the way, please?
•
• b. 반찬 좀 더 주실 수 있으세요?

Could you give me some
more side dishes, please?
•
• c. 저 좀 도와주실 수 있으세요?

# 제가 도와드릴까요?

❶ *Trace the sentences and practice your handwriting.*

제가 도와드릴까요?

제가 도와드릴까요?

❷ *Match the sentences.*

*May I lend it to you?* •

• a. 제가 도와드릴까요?

*May I help you?* •

• b. 제가 빌려드릴까요?

*May I take it out for you?* •

• c. 제가 꺼내 드릴까요?

❸ *Write the sentences.*

*May I help you?*

*No, it's fine.*

아니요, 괜찮아요.

❶ *Trace the sentences and practice your handwriting.*

저희 같이 구경해요.

저희 같이 구경해요.

❷ *Fill in the blanks.*

**저희** ∨ [ ][ ] ∨ **구경**(하다) + **-해요.**

↑

[Adverb]
Together.

❸ *Find a new word from a dictionary and make your own sentence.*

① *It is a verb. (Write in basic form ending in 다)*
② *I'm suggesting you do this with me.*

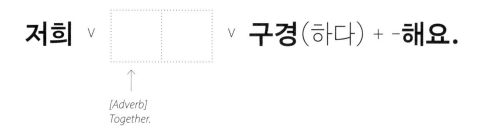

**저희 같이** 운동하다 **- 아 / 어 /(해)요.**

저희 같이 운동해요 **.**

# 아무거나 시켜도 돼요?

❶ *Trace the sentences and practice your handwriting.*

아무거나 시켜도 돼요?

아무거나 시켜도 돼요?

❷ *Match the sentences.*

*Is it okay
if I order anything?*

*Is it okay if I call anyone?*

*Is it okay
if I do it any way I want?*

a. 아무나 불러도 돼요?

b. 아무렇게나 해도 돼요?

c. 아무거나 시켜도 돼요?

❸ *Write the sentences.*

*Is it okay if I order anything?*

*No.*

안 돼요.

❶ *Trace the sentences and practice your handwriting.*

일 이 삼 사 오 육 칠 팔 구 십

일 이 삼 사 오 육 칠 팔 구 십

❷ *Match the numbers.*

17 •

3 •

75 •

a. **칠십오**

b. **삼**

c. **십칠**

❸ *Write the sentences. (Sino-Korean number)*

*How much is this?*

이거 얼마예요?

*It's 2,500 won.*

원이에요.

# 하나부터 열까지

**❶** *Trace the sentences and practice your handwriting.*

하나 둘 셋 넷 다섯 여섯 일곱 여덟 아홉 열

하나 둘 셋 넷 다섯 여섯 일곱 여덟 아홉 열

**❷** *Match the numbers.*

53 •                          • a. **쉰셋**

20 •                          • b. **열여섯**

16 •                          • c. **스물**

**❸** *Write the sentences. (native Korean number)*

*How old are you?*

몇 살이에요?

*I'm 24-years-old.*

살이에요.

# 달력 보기 (년/월/일)

❶ *Trace the sentences and practice your handwriting.*

이천삼십사 년 오월 이십사 일 수요일

이천삼십사 년 오월 이십사 일 수요일

❷ *Match the numbers.*

6/25 •

10/3 •

3/27 •

• a. 시월 삼 일

• b. 삼월 이십칠 일

• c. 유월 이십오 일

❸ *Write the sentences. (the date)*

*What month and day is it tomorrow?*

내일은 몇 월 며칠이에요?

*It's 10/9 tomorrow.*

내일은     월     일이에요.

# 시계 보기 (시/분/초)

**❶** *Trace the sentences and practice your handwriting.*

열 시 이십오 분 사십 초

열 시 이십오 분 사십 초

**❷** *Match the numbers.*

3:15 •                              • a. 세 시 십오 분

5:45 •                              • b. 오후 두 시

14:00 •                              • c. 다섯 시 사십오 분

**❸** *Write the sentences. (the time)*

*What time is it now?*

지금 몇 시예요?

*It's 11:20 now.*

지금       시       분이에요.

# 단위 명사

❶ *Trace the sentences and practice your handwriting.*

개 잔 병 권 명 분 마 리

개 잔 병 권 명 분 마 리

❷ *Look at the pictures and write in Korean.*

 가방 다섯 개

 고양이

 사람

 커피

 선생님

 책

 맥주

# 뭐 해요?

**❶** *Trace the sentences and practice your handwriting.*

뭐 해요?

뭐 해요?

**❷** *Fill in the blank.*

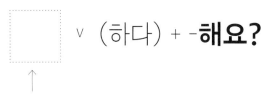

˅ (하다) + -**해요?**

↑

[Pronoun]
*Referring to an unknown fact or object.*
*What.*

**❸** *Look at the pictures and write in Korean as in the main book.*

| *To eat* | *To do* | *To drink* | *To see* |
|---|---|---|---|
| | | | |

# 여기 뭐가 맛있어요?

**❶** *Trace the sentences and practice your handwriting.*

여기 뭐가 맛있어요?

여기 뭐가 맛있어요?

**❷** *Match the sentences.*

What's in here? ●

What's delicious here? ●

What's popular here? ●

● a. 여기 뭐가 들어 있어요?

● b. 여기 뭐가 맛있어요?

● c. 여기 뭐가 잘 나가요?

**❸** *Write the sentences.*

*What's delicious here?*

*The iced latte is very popular.*

아이스 라테가 잘 나가요.

**1** *Trace the sentences and practice your handwriting.*

이거 얼마예요?

이거 얼마예요?

**2** *Look at the pictures and write the words in Korean.*

this thing

the thing

that thing

**3** *Write the sentences.*

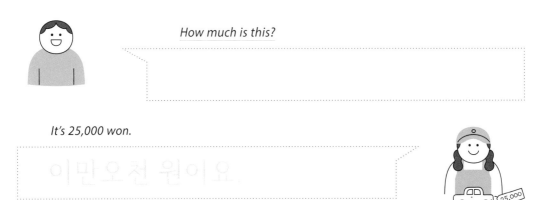

How much is this?

It's 25,000 won.

이만오천 원이요.

❶ *Trace the sentences and practice your handwriting.*

언제 가요?

언제 가요?

❷ *Fill in the blanks.*

 ∨ **가**(다) + **-아요?**

↑

[Pronoun]
*Referring to a time when one is unsure.*
*When.*

❸ *Match the sentences.*

| | |
|---|---|
| When are you going? ● | ● a. 언제 시작해요? |
| When does it start? ● | ● b. 언제 가요? |
| When does it end? ● | ● c. 언제 끝나요? |

# 버스 언제 와요?

❶ *Trace the sentences and practice your handwriting.*

버스 언제 와요?

버스 언제 와요?

❷ *Match the sentences.*

When does the subway come? •                    • a. 택시 언제 와요?

When does the bus come? •                        • b. 지하철 언제 와요?

When does the taxi come? •                        • c. 버스 언제 와요?

❸ *Find a new word from a dictionary and make your own sentence.*

①  *It is a noun.*
②  *I wonder when this will come.*

언제 와요?

?

❶ *Trace the sentences and practice your handwriting.*

여기가 어디예요?

여기가 어디예요?

❷ *Fill in the blanks.*

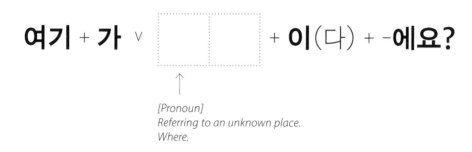

**여기** + **가** ∨ ⬚⬚ + **이**(**다**) + **-에요?**

↑

[Pronoun]
*Referring to an unknown place.*
*Where.*

❸ *Look at the pictures and write the words in Korean.*

*this place*

*the place*

*that place*

❶ *Trace the sentences and practice your handwriting.*

화장실은 어디에 있어요?

화장실은 어디에 있어요?

❷ *Look at the pictures and write the words in Korean.*

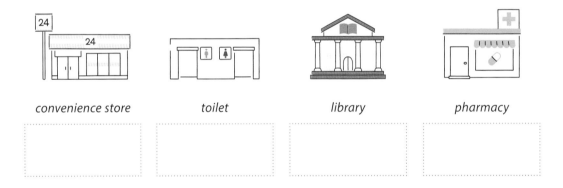

| convenience store | toilet | library | pharmacy |
|---|---|---|---|

❸ *Find a new word from a dictionary and make your own sentence.*

① *It is a noun.*
② *I wonder where this is.*

**은 / 는  어디에 있어요?**

**?**

❶ *Trace the sentences and practice your handwriting.*

주 문 은   어 디 에 서   해 요 ?

주 문 은   어 디 에 서   해 요 ?

❷ *Match the sentences.*

*Where can I take the bus?* •

• a. 주문은 어디에서 해요?

*Where can I buy water?* •

• b. 버스는 어디에서 타요?

*Where can I place an order?* •

• c. 물은 어디에서 사요?

❸ *Write the sentences.*

*Where can I place an order?*

*Do it here, please.*

여기에서 하세요.

# 택배는 어떻게 보내요?

❶ *Trace the sentences and practice your handwriting.*

택배는 어떻게 보내요?

택배는 어떻게 보내요?

❷ *Fill in the blanks.*

**택배** + **는** ∨ [　　　][　　] ∨ **보내**(다) + **-어요?**

↑

*[Adverb]*
*By what means or method.*
*How.*

❸ *Look at the pictures and write in Korean as in the main book.*

| Send a package. | Close the window. | Open the door. | Throw the trash away. |

❶ *Trace the sentences and practice your handwriting.*

왜 그래요?

왜 그래요?

❷ *Fill in the blank.*

∨ **그래** + **요?**

↑

[Adverb]
For what reason.
Why.

❸ *Write the sentences.*

*Why are you like that?*

*Because the kimchi is too spicy.*

김치가 너무 매워서요.

❶ *Trace the sentences and practice your handwriting.*

이분은 누구세요?

이분은 누구세요?

❷ *Look at the pictures and write the words in Korean.*

*this person (honorific)*

*the person (honorific)*

*that person (honorific)*

❸ *Write the sentences.*

*Who is this person?*

*She is a teacher.*

그분은 선생님이에요.

❶ *Trace the sentences and practice your handwriting.*

누가 제일 잘해요?

누가 제일 잘해요?

❷ *Fill in the blanks.*

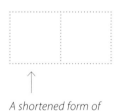

∨ **제일** ∨ **잘**(하다) + **-해요?**

↑

*A shortened form of*
'**누구+가**(who is)'

❸ *Match the sentences.*

| | |
|---|---|
| *Who is the most fun?* ● | ● a. 누가 제일 귀여워요? |
| *Who is the best?* ● | ● b. 누가 제일 재미있어요? |
| *Who is the cutest?* ● | ● c. 누가 제일 잘해요? |

**❶** *Trace the sentences and practice your handwriting.*

네.

네.

**❷** *Match the sentences.*

Good.  ●                    ●  a. 네.

Yes.  ●                    ●  b. 좋아요.

Right.  ●                    ●  c. 맞아요.

**❸** *Write the sentences.*

*Do you live in Seoul?*

서울에 살아요?

*Yes, I live in Seoul.*

❶ *Trace the sentences and practice your handwriting.*

아니요.

아니요.

❷ *Fill in the blank.*

아니 + [    ] **.**

↑

*Indicates respect to the listener.*

❸ *Match the sentences.*

No.　　●

I can't.　　●

It's okay.　　●

●　a. **안 돼요.**

●　b. **아니요.**

●　c. **괜찮아요.**

# 그냥 그래요.

❶ *Trace the sentences and practice your handwriting.*

그냥 그래요.

그냥 그래요.

❷ *Match the sentences.*

*So-so.* ●                    ● a. 별로예요.

*Not really.* ●                 ● b. 그냥 그래요.

*I don't know well either.* ●       ● c. 저도 잘 몰라요.

❸ *Write the sentences.*

*The coffee here is delicious?*

어기 커피 맛있어요?

*So-so.*

**①** *Trace the sentences and practice your handwriting.*

잠깐만요.

잠깐만요.

**②** *Fill in the blanks.*

↑
*[Noun]*
*For a very short period of time.*

**③** *Match the sentences.*

| | | |
|---|---|---|
| *Just ten more minutes.* ● | ● | a. 10분만요. |
| *Wait a second.* ● | ● | b. 잠깐만요. |
| *Please wait a moment.* ● | ● | c. 잠깐만 기다려 주세요. |

# 그러니까요.

**❶** *Trace the sentences and practice your handwriting.*

그러니까요.

그러니까요.

**❷** *Match the sentences.*

Tell me about it. ⬤ ⬤ a. 제 말이요.

It happens. ⬤ ⬤ b. 그럴 수 있어요.

That's what I am saying. ⬤ ⬤ c. 그러니까요.

**❸** *Write the sentences.*

*The side dishes here are great.*

여기 반찬 맛있어요.

*Tell me about it!*

❶ *Trace the sentences and practice your handwriting.*

여기요.

여기요.

❷ *Fill in the blanks.*

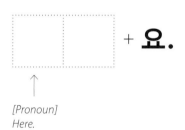

↑
[Pronoun]
Here.

+ **요.**

❸ *Write the sentences.*

*Give me your passport, please.*

여권 주세요.

*Here it is.*

# 진짜요?

**1** *Trace the sentences and practice your handwriting.*

진짜요?

진짜요?

**2** *Match the sentences.*

Really?  •                         •   a. 그래요?

What did you say?  •               •   b. 진짜요?

Is it?  •                           •   c. 뭐라고요?

**3** *Write the sentences.*

I came from New York.

저는 뉴욕에서 왔어요.

Really?

❶ *Trace the sentences and practice your handwriting.*

저 친구 만났어요.

저 친구 만났어요.

❷ *Fill in the blank.*

저 ∨ 친구 ∨ 만나(다) + - [ ] - + -어요.

↑

[Ending]
*Expresses the past tense.*

❸ *Match the sentences.*

I made a friend.　　　●

I met a friend.　　　●

I needed a friend.　　　●

●　a. 저 친구 필요했어요.

●　b. 저 친구 만들었어요.

●　c. 저 친구 만났어요.

# 그 사람은 경찰이었어요.

**❶** *Trace the sentences and practice your handwriting.*

그 사람은 경찰이었어요.

그 사람은 경찰이었어요.

**❷** *Match the sentences.*

This person was
a teacher.

a. 저 사람은 남자 친구였어요.

That person was
my boyfriend.

b. 이 사람은 선생님이었어요.

The person was
a police officer.

c. 그 사람은 경찰이었어요.

**❸** *Find a new word from a dictionary and make your own sentence.*

① *It is a noun.*
② *That person was this.*

그 사람은 [            ] -이었어요 / 였어요 .

[                              ] .

❶ *Trace the sentences and practice your handwriting.*

지금 티브이 보고 있어요.

지금 티브이 보고 있어요.

❷ *Fill in the blanks.*

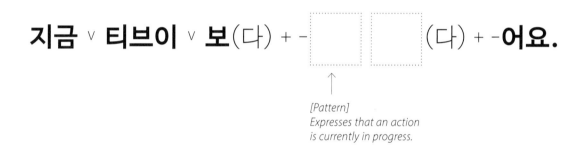

지금 ∨ 티브이 ∨ 보(다) + - [　] [　] (다) + -**어요.**

↑

[Pattern]
*Expresses that an action
is currently in progress.*

❸ *Look at the pictures and write in Korean as in the main book.*

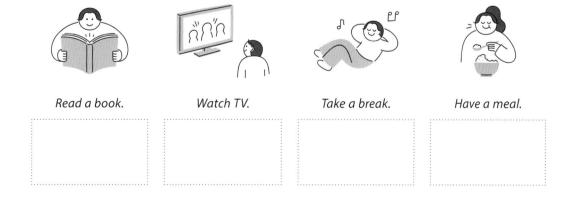

| *Read a book.* | *Watch TV.* | *Take a break.* | *Have a meal.* |

# 이건 내일 할 거예요.

❶ *Trace the sentences and practice your handwriting.*

이건 내일 할 거예요.

이건 내일 할 거예요.

❷ *Match the sentences.*

I will do this tomorrow.             a. 이 옷은 내일 입을 거예요.

I will visit this famous restaurant tomorrow.     b. 이건 내일 할 거예요.

I will wear this clothes tomorrow.       c. 이 맛집은 내일 찾아갈 거예요.

❸ *Write the sentences.*

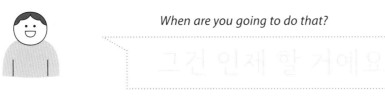

*When are you going to do that?*

그건 언제 할 거예요?

*I will do this tomorrow.*

❶ *Trace the sentences and practice your handwriting.*

저는 한국어도 배워요.

저는 한국어도 배워요.

❷ *Fill in the blank.*

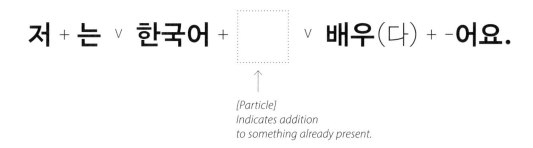

저 + 는 ∨ 한국어 + [　] ∨ 배우(다) + -어요.

↑
*[Particle]*
*Indicates addition*
*to something already present.*

❸ *Find a new word from a dictionary and make your own sentence.*

① *It is a noun.*
② *I also learn this.*

저는 [　　　　　] 도 배워요.

[　　　　　　　　　　　　　　　　　　] .

# 저는 영어만 가르쳐요.

**❶** *Trace the sentences and practice your handwriting.*

저는 영어만 가르쳐요.

저는 영어만 가르쳐요.

**❷** *Fill in the blank.*

**저** + **는** ∨ **영어** + [    ] ∨ **가르치**(**다**) + -**어요.**

↑
*[Particle]*
*Indicates specifying*
*something exclusively.*

**❸** *Match the sentences.*

| | |
|---|---|
| *I teach only English.* ● | ● a. 저는 영어만 가르쳐요. |
| *Only my wife teaches English.* ● | ● b. 아내도 영어만 가르쳐요. |
| *My wife teaches only English, too.* ● | ● c. 아내만 영어를 가르쳐요. |

❶ *Trace the sentences and practice your handwriting.*

연필하고 지우개하고 가져오세요.

연필하고 지우개하고 가져오세요.

❷ *Look at the pictures and write in Korean as in the main book.*

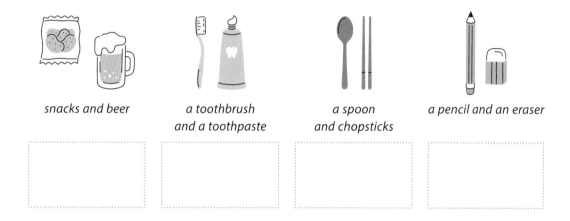

| snacks and beer | a toothbrush and a toothpaste | a spoon and chopsticks | a pencil and an eraser |

❸ *Find a new word from a dictionary and make your own sentence.*

① *They are nouns.*
② *I'm asking you to bring this and that.*

＿＿＿＿하고 ＿＿＿＿하고 가져오세요.

＿＿＿＿＿＿＿＿＿＿＿＿＿＿＿＿.

# 저한테 물어보세요.

❶ *Trace the sentences and practice your handwriting.*

저한테 물어보세요.

저한테 물어보세요.

❷ *Fill in the blanks.*

저 + [    ] ∨ 물어보(다) + -시- + -어요.

↑
*[Particle]*
*Indicates who an action*
*is for or directed towards.*

❸ *Find a new word from a dictionary and make your own sentence.*

→ ① *It is a verb that implies some movement. (Write in basic form ending in 다)*
② *I'm telling you to do this to me.*

저한테 [        ] -시 / 으시- 어요.

[                                                            ] •

❶ *Trace the sentences and practice your handwriting.*

저는 친구랑 놀았어요.

저는 친구랑 놀았어요.

❷ *Fill in the blank.*

**저** + **는** ∨ **친구** + [　　] ∨ **놀**(다) + **-았-** + **-어요.**

↑

*[Particle]*
*Indicates a companion*
*involved in an action.*

❸ *Match the sentences.*

I had a fight
with my friend.　　●

I made a promise
with my friends.　　●

I hung out
with my friend.　　●

●　a. 저는 친구랑 놀았어요.

●　b. 저는 친구랑 싸웠어요.

●　c. 저는 친구들이랑 약속했어요.

# 집으로 가는 길이에요.

❶ *Trace the sentences and practice your handwriting.*

집으로 가는 길이에요.

집으로 가는 길이에요.

❷ *Look at the pictures and write the words in Korean.*

| bar | house | airport | school |
|-----|-------|---------|--------|
|     |       |         |        |

❸ *Find a new word from a dictionary and make your own sentence.*

① *It is a noun.*
② *I'm on my way to here.*

로 / 으로   가는 길이에요.

# 그분은 한국인이 아니에요.

❶ *Trace the sentences and practice your handwriting.*

그분은 한국인이 아니에요.

그분은 한국인이 아니에요.

❷ *Match the sentences.*

He/she is not
a rich person.　●

He/she is not Korean.　●

He/she is not a fool.　●

　●　a. 그분은 부자가 아니에요.

　●　b. 그분은 바보가 아니에요.

　●　c. 그분은 한국인이 아니에요.

❸ *Find a new word from a dictionary and make your own sentence.*

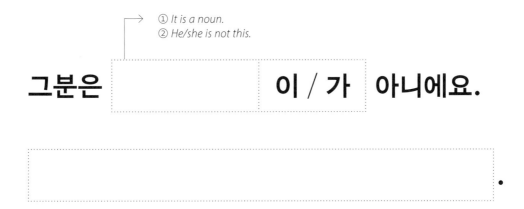

① *It is a noun.*
② *He/she is not this.*

그분은 [          ] 이 / 가 아니에요.

[                                                    ] .

❶ *Trace the sentences and practice your handwriting.*

저는 안 힘들어요.

저는 안 힘들어요.

❷ *Fill in the blank.*

저 + 는 ∨ ☐ ∨ 힘들(다) + -어요.

↑

[Adverb]
Not.

❸ *Match the sentences.*

| | |
|---|---|
| *I'm not busy.* ● | ● a. 저는 안 힘들어요. |
| *We are not close.* ● | ● b. 저는 안 바빠요. |
| *I'm not tired.* ● | ● c. 저희는 안 친해요. |

❶ *Trace the sentences and practice your handwriting.*

저는 못 걸어요.

저는 못 걸어요.

❷ *Fill in the blank.*

**저** + **는** ∨ [　　] ∨ **걷**(다) + **-어요.**

↑

[Adverb]
Cannot.

❸ *Find a new word from a dictionary and make your own sentence.*

① *It is a verb. (Write in basic form ending in* 다)
② *I can't do this.*

**저는 못** [　　] **-아 / 어/ 해 요.**

[　　　　　　　　　　　　　　　　] .

# 늦지 마세요.

❶ *Trace the sentences and practice your handwriting.*

늦지 마세요.

늦지 마세요.

❷ *Look at the pictures and write in Korean as in the main book.*

*Don't run.*

*Don't leave it.*

*Don't be late.*

*Don't change it.*

❸ *Write the sentences.*

*Let's meet at 10 o'clock tomorrow.*

내일 10시에 만나요.

*Good. Don't be late.*

좋아요.

# 기다릴게요.

**❶** *Trace the sentences and practice your handwriting.*

기다릴게요.

기다릴게요.

**❷** *Match the sentences.*

I will wait.　　　　●

I will be right back.　●

I will order.　　　　●

　　　　● a. **다녀올게요.**

　　　　● b. **기다릴게요.**

　　　　● c. **주문할게요.**

**❸** *Find a new word from a dictionary and make your own sentence.*

　　　　① *It is a a verb. (Write in basic form ending in* 다*)*
　　　　② *I'm telling you I will do this.*

| | -ㄹ게 / 을게 요. |

　　　　　　　　　　　　　　　　　　　　　　　　●

# 한번 시도해 보세요.

**❶** *Trace the sentences and practice your handwriting.*

한번 시도해 보세요.

한번 시도해 보세요.

**❷** *Fill in the blanks.*

**한번** ∨ **시도**(하다) + - ☐ ☐ (다) + -**시**- + -**어요.**

↑

[Pattern]
*Expresses trying something out.*

**❸** *Match the sentences.*

*Just think about it.* •               • a. 한번 시도해 보세요.

*Just try smiling.* •               • b. 한번 웃어 보세요.

*Just give it a try.* •               • c. 한번 생각해 보세요.

❶ *Trace the sentences and practice your handwriting.*

놀이공원 가 본 적 있으세요?

놀이공원 가 본 적 있으세요?

❷ *Match the sentences.*

Have you ever been
to the dentist?

Have you ever been
to an amusement park?

Have you ever been
to a singing room?

a. 놀이공원 가 본 적 있으세요?

b. 치과 가 본 적 있으세요?

c. 노래방 가 본 적 있으세요?

❸ *Find a new word from a dictionary and make your own sentence.*

① *It is a noun.*
② *I'm asking you if you have been here.*

**가 본 적 있으세요?**

?

# 저 한국말 할 수 있어요.

❶ *Trace the sentences and practice your handwriting.*

저 한국말 할 수 있어요.

저 한국말 할 수 있어요.

❷ *Fill in the blanks.*

**저** ᵛ **한국말** ᵛ **하**(다) + - [    ] [    ] **있**(다) + -**어요.**

↑

[Pattern]
*Expresses the ability to do something.*

❸ *Look at the pictures and write in Korean as in the main book.*

| Fly in the sky. | Drive. | Cook doenjang jjigae. | Speak Korean. |

# 좀 싱거운 것 같아요.

❶ *Trace the sentences and practice your handwriting.*

좀 싱거운 것 같아요.

좀 싱거운 것 같아요.

❷ *Look at the pictures and write in Korean as in the main book.*

| *(It's) Big.* | *(It's) Small.* | *(It's) Bland.* | *(It's) Hot.* |
|---|---|---|---|

❸ *Find a new word from a dictionary and make your own sentence.*

① *It is a a verb or an adjective. (Write in basic form ending in 다)*
② *I'm indirectly saying that it seems this way.*

## 좀 [        ] -는 / ㄴ / 은 것 같아요.

[                    ] .

# 잘 모르겠어요.

❶ *Trace the sentences and practice your handwriting.*

잘 모르겠어요.

잘 모르겠어요.

❷ *Match the sentences.*

I think I understand well.　●

　●　a. 잘 모르겠어요.

I think I can't stand it.　●

　●　b. 못 참겠어요.

I think I don't know well.　●

　●　c. 잘 알겠어요.

❸ *Write the sentences.*

*Is this spicy?*

이거 매워요?

*I think I don't know well.*

# 백화점에 옷 사러 가요.

❶ *Trace the sentences and practice your handwriting.*

백화점에 옷 사러 가요.

백화점에 옷 사러 가요.

❷ *Fill in the blank.*

**백화점** + **에** ∨ **옷** ∨ **사**(다) + - [　] ∨ **가**(다) + -**아요.**

↑

*[Ending]*
*Expresses the purpose*
*of going or coming actions.*

❸ *Find a new word from a dictionary and make your own sentence.*

① *It is a noun.*
② *I'm going to the department store to buy this.*

**백화점에** [　] **사러 가요.**

[　] .

# 내일 만나기로 했어요.

❶ *Trace the sentences and practice your handwriting.*

내일 만나기로 했어요.

내일 만나기로 했어요.

❷ *Match the sentences.*

We decided to
meet tomorrow.

I decided to wash
tomorrow.

I decided to wash
my hair tomorrow.

a. 내일 씻기로 했어요.

b. 머리는 내일 감기로 했어요.

c. 내일 만나기로 했어요.

❸ *Write the sentences.*

*When are you going to meet your friend?*

친구 언제 만나기로 했어요?

*We decided to meet tomorrow.*

❶ *Trace the sentences and practice your handwriting.*

오늘은 찜닭이 먹고 싶어요.

오늘은 찜닭이 먹고 싶어요.

❷ *Fill in the blanks.*

**찜닭** + **이** ∨ **먹**(다) + - ☐ ☐ (다) + -**어요.**

↑

*[Pattern]*
*Expresses a desire to do something.*

❸ *Find a new word from a dictionary and make your own sentence.*

① *It is a noun.*
② *I want to eat this today.*

**오늘은** ☐ **이 / 가 먹고 싶어요.**

_____ •

# 진짜 힘들어요.

❶ *Trace the sentences and practice your handwriting.*

진짜 힘들어요.

진짜 힘들어요.

❷ *Fill in the blanks.*

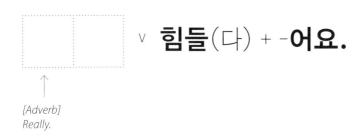

∨ **힘들**(다) + **-어요.**

↑

*[Adverb]*
*Really.*

❸ *Write the sentences.*

*Are you okay?*

괜찮아요?

*I'm really tired.*

# 완전(히) 멋있어요.

❶ *Trace the sentences and practice your handwriting.*

완전 멋있어요.

완전 멋있어요.

❷ *Match the sentences.*

She's so lovely.　　　　●　　　　　　　　●　a. 완전 멋있어요.

It's so cool.　　　●　　　　　　　　●　b. 완전 잘생겼어요.

He's so handsome.　　●　　　　　　　　●　c. 완전 사랑스러워요.

❸ *Find a new word from a dictionary and make your own sentence.*

　　　　　　① *It is a verb or an adjective. (Write in basic form ending in* 다*)*
　　　　　　② *I think it is so like this.*

**완전** [　　　　]　　-**아 / 어 / 해 요.**

[　　　　　　　　　　　　　　　　　　　　　　]**.**

# 너무 비싸요.

❶ *Trace the sentences and practice your handwriting.*

너무 비싸요.

너무 비싸요.

❷ *Look at the pictures and write in Korean as in the main book.*

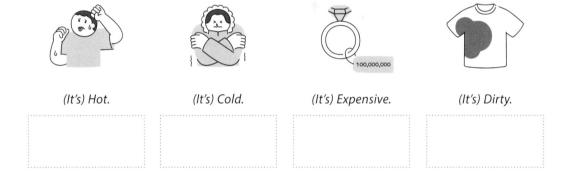

(It's) Hot.　　　　(It's) Cold.　　　　(It's) Expensive.　　　　(It's) Dirty.

❸ *Find a new word from a dictionary and make your own sentence.*

① *It is a verb or an adjective. (Write in basic form ending in* 다*)*
② *I think it is too much like this.*

너무 [　　　　] -아 / 어 / 해 요.

[　　　　　　　　　　　　　　　　　　　　　　] .

❶ *Trace the sentences and practice your handwriting.*

빨리 타요.

빨리 타요.

❷ *Fill in the blanks.*

| | |
|---|---|

∨ **타**(다) + **-아요.**

↑

*[Adverb]*
*Quickly.*

❸ *Match the sentences.*

*Get on quickly.* ● ● a. 빨리 자요.

*Come slowly.* ● ● b. 빨리 타요.

*Go to sleep quickly.* ● ● c. 천천히 와요.

❶ *Trace the sentences and practice your handwriting.*

혹시 펜 있으세요?

혹시 펜 있으세요?

❷ *Fill in the blanks.*

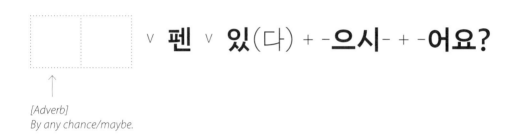

∨ **펜** ∨ **있**(다) + **-으시-** + **-어요?**

↑

*[Adverb]*
*By any chance/maybe.*

❸ *Look at the pictures and write the words in Korean.*

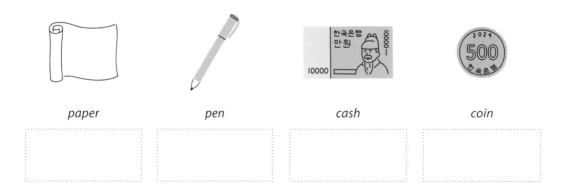

| paper | pen | cash | coin |
| --- | --- | --- | --- |
|  |  |  |  |

# 갑자기 비가 와요.

❶ *Trace the sentences and practice your handwriting.*

갑자기 비가 와요.

갑자기 비가 와요.

❷ *Match the sentences.*

*Suddenly it's raining.* •          • a. 갑자기 눈이 와요.

*Suddenly it's snowing.* •          • b. 갑자기 비가 와요.

*Suddenly something came up.* •          • c. 갑자기 일이 생겼어요.

❸ *Find a new word from a dictionary and make your own sentence.*

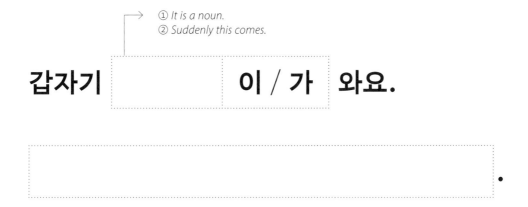

① *It is a noun.*
② *Suddenly this comes.*

**갑자기** _____ **이 / 가 와요.**

_____ .

# 그냥 해 봐요.

❶ *Trace the sentences and practice your handwriting.*

그냥 해 봐요.

그냥 해 봐요.

❷ *Match the sentences.*

Just try it. ◦                    ◦ a. 혼자 해 봐요.

Try it by yourself. ◦              ◦ b. 다시 해 봐요.

Try again. ◦                      ◦ c. 그냥 해 봐요.

❸ *Write the sentences.*

*Do you think I can do it?*

제가 할 수 있을까요?

*Just try it.*

# WORKBOOK ANSWERS

## 1. GREETINGS

p. 2   **2.** 시   **3.** 안녕하세요?

p. 3   **2.** ㅂ니다   **3.** b/c/a

p. 4   **2.** b/a/c   **3.** 죄송합니다.

p. 5   **2.** 겠

     **3.** 맛있게 드세요./ 잘 먹었습니다./
배불러요./ 잘 먹겠습니다.

p. 6   **2.** b/a/c   **3.** 안녕히 계세요.

p. 7   **2.** 어요   **3.** b/c/a

p. 8   **2.** 에요   **3.** 예 저는 소피아예요.

## 2. PARTICLE ①

p. 9   **2.** a/c/b   **3.** 언니/오빠/형/누나

p. 10   **2.** 를   **3.** 예 저는 초콜릿을 먹어요.

p. 11   **2.** 가   **3.** 김밥/커피/라면/불고기

p. 12   **2.** 에   **3.** 예 저는 시카고에 살아요.

p. 13   **2.** 밤/아침/저녁/점심

     **3.** 저는 아침에 운동해요.

p. 14   **2.** 에서   **3.** 예 저는 이탈리아에서 왔어요.

## 3. MAKING A REQUEST

p. 15   **2.** 우산/가방/여권/휴대폰

     **3.** 예 신발 주세요.

p. 16   **2.** c/a/b   **3.** 이거 계산해 주세요.

p. 17   **2.** 안   **3.** c/a/b

p. 18   **2.** 소금을 넣어요./ 견과류를 빼요./
설탕을 넣어요./ 시럽을 빼요.

     **3.** 예 후추 넣어 주시겠어요?

p. 19   **2.** 좀   **3.** c/a/b

p. 20   **2.** b/a/c   **3.** 제가 도와드릴까요?

p. 21   **2.** 같이

     **3.** 예 운동하다/ 저희 같이 운동해요.

p. 22   **2.** c/a/b   **3.** 아무거나 시켜도 돼요?

## 4. NUMBERS

p. 23   **2.** c/b/a   **3.** 이천오백 원이에요

p. 24   **2.** a/c/b   **3.** 스물네 살이에요

p. 25   **2.** c/a/b   **3.** 내일은 시월 구 일이에요

p. 26   **2.** a/c/b   **3.** 지금 열한 시 이십 분이에요

p. 27   **2.** 가방 다섯 개/ 고양이 세 마리/
사람 여섯 명/ 커피 여덟 잔/ 선생님 한 분/
책 열두 권/ 맥주 아홉 병

## 5. ASKING QUESTIONS

p. 28   **2.** 뭐

     **3.** 먹어요./ 해요./ 마셔요./ 봐요.

p. 29   **2.** a/b/c   **3.** 여기 뭐가 맛있어요?

p. 30   **2.** 이거/그거/저거   **3.** 이거 얼마예요?

p. 31   **2.** 언제   **3.** b/a/c

p. 32   **2.** b/c/a   **3.** 예 비행기 언제 와요?

p. 33   **2.** 어디   **3.** 여기/거기/저기

p. 34   **2.** 편의점/화장실/도서관/약국

     **3.** 예 학교는 어디에 있어요?

p. 35   **2.** b/c/a   **3.** 주문은 어디에서 해요?

p. 36   **2.** 어떻게

     **3.** 택배를 보내요./ 창문을 닫아요./
문을 열어요./ 쓰레기를 버려요.

p. 37   **2.** 왜   **3.** 왜 그래요?

p. 38   **2.** 이분/그분/저분   **3.** 이분은 누구세요?

p. 39   **2.** 누가   **3.** b/c/a

## 6. RESPONSES

p. 40   **2.** b/a/c   **3.** 네, 저는 서울에 살아요.

p. 41   **2.** 요   **3.** b/a/c

p. 42   **2.** b/a/c   **3.** 그냥 그래요.

p. 43   **2.** 잠깐   **3.** a/b/c

p. 44   **2.** c/b/a   **3.** 그러니까요!

p. 45  **2.** 여기  **3.** 여기요.

p. 46  **2.** b/c/a  **3.** 진짜요?

## 7. TENSES

p. 47  **2.** 았  **3.** b/c/a

p. 48  **2.** b/a/c  **3.** ⑩ 그 사람은 의사였어요.

p. 49  **2.** 고 있

**3.** 책 읽어요./ 티브이 봐요./

쉬어요./ 밥 먹어요.

p. 50  **2.** b/c/a  **3.** 이건 내일 할 거예요.

## 8. PARTICLE ②

p. 51  **2.** 도  **3.** ⑩ 저는 중국어도 배워요.

p. 52  **2.** 만  **3.** a/c/b

p. 53  **2.** 과자하고 맥주/

칫솔하고 치약/

숟가락하고 젓가락/

연필하고 지우개

**3.** ⑩ 공책하고 펜하고 가져오세요.

p. 54  **2.** 한테

**3.** ⑩ 보내다/ 저한테 보내세요.

p. 55  **2.** 랑  **3.** b/c/a

p. 56  **2.** 술집/집/공항/학교

**3.** ⑩ 회사로 가는 길이에요.

## 9. NEGATION

p. 57  **2.** a/c/b

**3.** ⑩ 그분은 선생님이 아니에요.

p. 58  **2.** 안  **3.** b/c/a

p. 59  **2.** 못  **3.** ⑩ 읽다/ 저는 못 읽어요.

p. 60  **2.** 뛰지 마세요./ 남기지 마세요./

늦지 마세요./ 바꾸지 마세요.

**3.** 늦지 마세요.

## 10. EXPRESSIONS

p. 61  **2.** b/a/c  **3.** ⑩ 연락하다/ 연락할게요.

p. 62  **2.** 해 보  **3.** c/b/a

p. 63  **2.** b/a/c  **3.** ⑩ 영화관 가 본 적 있으세요?

p. 64  **2.** ㄹ 수

**3.** 하늘을 날아요./ 운전을 해요./

된장찌개를 끓여요./ 한국말을 해요.

p. 65  **2.** 커요./ 작아요./ 싱거워요./ 뜨거워요.

**3.** ⑩ 더럽다/ 좀 더러운 것 같아요.

p. 66  **2.** c/b/a  **3.** 잘 모르겠어요.

p. 67  **2.** 러  **3.** ⑩ 백화점에 바지 사러 가요.

p. 68  **2.** c/a/b  **3.** 내일 만나기로 했어요.

p. 69  **2.** 고 싶

**3.** ⑩ 오늘은 고기가 먹고 싶어요.

## 11. USING ADVERBS

p. 70  **2.** 진짜  **3.** 진짜 힘들어요.

p.71  **2.** c/a/b

**3.** ⑩ 부드럽다/ 완전 부드러워요.

p. 72  **2.** 더워요./ 추워요./ 비싸요./ 더러워요.

**3.** ⑩ 느리다/ 너무 느려요.

p. 73  **2.** 빨리  **3.** b/c/a

p. 74  **2.** 혹시  **3.** 종이/펜/현금/동전

p. 75  **2.** b/a/c  **3.** ⑩ 갑자기 친구가 와요.

p. 76  **2.** c/a/b  **3.** 그냥 해 봐요.